The Inner Guard

and

The Deacons

.

The Inner Guard

and

The Deacons

Charles J. Carter

LONDON

LEWIS MASONIC

Further book by the same author
The Director of Ceremonies

British Library Cataloguing in Publication Data
Carter, Charles J.
 The Inner Guard and The Deacons.
 1. Greater Britain. Freemasonry. Officers
 I. Title
 336.10941
ISBN 0 85318 174 8

First Published in England in 1990
by Lewis Masonic, Ian Allan Regalia Ltd, who are members of the Ian Allan Group of Companies, Terminal House, Shepperton TW17 8AS

Phototypesetting/Printing:
Ian Allan Printing Ltd, Coombelands House, Addlestone, Weybridge, Surrey.

Contents

THE INNER GUARD

THE DEACONS

Unless otherwise indicated the ritual passages in this book are based on Emulation. There will be slight variations in other rituals.

THE
INNER
GUARD

About The Author

CHARLES JAMES CARTER was initiated into the Three Pillars Lodge No 4923 in May 1962, became Master in 1971 and Secretary the following year. In 1971 he became Founding Secretary of the Plantagenets Lodge No 8409 in the Province of Kent and Master in 1973. He served the office of Preceptor and Director of Ceremonies for ten years.

In 1977 he was promoted to Provincial Deputy Director of Ceremonies a rank he was to hold for ten years before being promoted to Assistant Provincial Grand Master (West Kent) in 1987.

He is a member of several lodges and Chapters in Kent including the West Kent Provincial Grand Stewards' Lodge No 8565 (eight years as Director of Ceremonies); he is a founder and the present secretary of the Fiennes Cornwallis Lodge No 9279, the executive Lodge for the Province of West Kent. He was appointed to the rank of Past Assistant Grand Director of Ceremonies in 1981 and promoted to Past Senior Grand Deacon in 1988.

He is the current secretary of the Quatuor Coronati Correspondence Circle Limited, London, where he is responsible for the worldwide operations of the Correspondence Circle of the Quatuor Coronari Lodge, the premier Lodge of Research in the world.

Chapter 1:

Historical Preface

The Inner Guard developed in the eighteenth-century lodges from an Inner Tyler or Inner Garder, it being found that there was a particular need for an officer guarding the inside of the door under the direct instructions of the Junior Warden, whose particular duty it was and is to see that no unqualified person gains admission.

In effect he is a door Warden and in some of the early lodges he was at first a Serving Brother whose duties were closely concerned with those of the Tyler, who of course was also a Serving Brother.

The Inner Guard has his place in Irish and Scottish lodges but is unknown in most American lodges, in which the Junior Deacon, acting under the commands of the Junior Warden, admits Brethren and has a special responsibility for candidates and visitors.

This responsibility he is made to feel is a very real one indeed, to be shared between him and the Tyler.

The Inner Guard existed in fact in English lodges long before he was honoured with his particular name.

In 1734 the Old King's Arms Lodge No. 28 had a 'door-keeper' and it is likely that he was the youngest Entered Apprentice present and that he was armed with a trowel.

The first mention of the title Inner Guard can be accurately placed in the year 1799 as described by Bro. Norman Rogers in a paper "200 Years of Freemasonry in Bury" published in AQC LVIII, in which it is recorded that the Anchor and Hope Lodge appointed an Inner Guard.

The first mention of the office in the Book of Constitutions was in 1815 which makes the introduction of that office a rather late event in the English system.

Not until the turn of the century did the Inner Tyler, or 'doorkeeper', begin to be called the Guarder, or Guard, and not until about 1814 was there official recognition of the actual office of Inner Guard.

In such an old lodge as the Love and Honour No. 75, Falmouth, the first mention of Inner Guard is in the records of 1816, whilst the Burlington Lodge (founded 1756), now No. 96, first mentions the Inner Guard in the minutes of 1814.

Where the Inner Guard was a Serving Brother he was undoubtedly regarded as the Tyler's assistant, various old minutes making that position quite clear.

In the Lodge of Honour and Friendship, Blandford, that ceased to exist in 1838 (Blandford's present lodge of that name, No. 1266, dates back to 1869), a particular Brother was allowed one shilling for each lodge night "and one shilling for every newly initiated Brother to take on himself the office of Inner Guard and to assist the Tyler . . . . and initiated without fee".

The Royal Augustus Lodge of Monmouth (erased in 1830) had an Outer Tyler and a Junior Tyler.

The weapon with which the Inner Guard was armed, where tradition helps us in this respect, was the pointed trowel, and it is not apparently in keeping with oldest custom that he should be armed with a sword of any kind for that is the emblematic weapon of the Outer Guard, or Tyler.

Probably it was the Serving Brother Inner Guard's position as Junior to the Tyler that led to his also being armed with a sword, albeit a sheathed one, as contrasted with the drawn sword of the Tyler.

Grand Lodge authorized the Inner Guard's jewel — the crossed swords — in 1819 and in so doing set its seal upon a practice which, so far as can be seen, does not accord with the earliest custom.

Chapter 2:

The Office of Inner Guard

The purpose of this book is to examine the office of the Inner Guard in detail and set out, for the benefit of the brother appointed or aspiring to that office, the features that are particularly relevant to his performance of that role.

If the holder of this office takes the time and trouble to make himself familiar with the many facets of the post, and thereby fulfils that role well, he will undoubtedly bring credit to himself as well as satisfaction to the lodge, but perhaps more particularly to the Master by whom he was appointed.

The work of the Inner Guard has changed considerably over the past two hundred years and the role we expect a brother appointed to that office to perform is well known and accepted by all Freemasons operating under the United Grand Lodge of England.

Although the information contained in these pages will indicate the most generally used forms of ceremonial and verbiage it should be remembered that Preceptors of Lodges of Instruction may well indicate that the lodge for which they are responsible carries out a certain action or speaks a given phrase in a different way from that indicated herein. The reader is therefore cautioned to avoid using this book as a tool with which to prove a point or argue with a Preceptor.

The office of Inner Guard is one of those very few amongst the team of officers in a lodge which instigate actions or give instructions.

The holder of this office should therefore remember that he has a duty to ensure that he speaks clearly and at a level of audibility which can be heard both by the person to whom he is speaking as well as all the assembled brethren.

This fact applies particularly during his frequent exchanges with the Tyler during the working of the various degrees.

Chapter 3:

Poignard

The jewel of office handed to the Inner Guard on the occasion of his being appointed to that office is the Poignard.

The symbolic use of this instrument is well known but its origins appear to be derived from the custom of protection, namely the Tyler or Outer Guard having a Sword and the Inner Tyler or Guard having a similar sword.

Time, as well as custom and use, reduced the sword of the Inner Guard as he became known, to a figurative adornment at the end of his collar of office which Grand Lodge describe now as two swords of saltire, i.e., being two swords crossed right over left. Plate 44 of the Book of Constitutions shows this in fine detail.

The Poignard therefore, it would appear, can be any form of pointed instrument providing it produces the correct response from the Candidate on the night of his Initiation. Styles range from very ornate and be-jewelled models to very ordinary plain and inexpensive types.

There is no clearly laid-down pattern that shows the style or design which this appurtenance should follow.

It is suspected that, as with so many items of masonic furniture provided today, much of the design has been left to the suppliers or manufacturers of such items and that their design and subsequent cost have been established as a result of changing times and financial restrictions.

Chapter 4:

The Duties of the Inner Guard

Taken in their broadest sense the responsibilities cover the entry and exit of anyone who wishes to enter or leave the lodge once the door has been closed after the incoming procession has completed its entry.

From that point onwards it is clear that no one can enter or leave without the permission of the Worshipful Master, albeit that he does sometimes delegate that responsibility to his Junior Warden, particularly in regard to the entry of brethren arriving after the meeting has commenced.

The Inner Guard takes his instructions from either the Worshipful Master or the Junior Warden and, dependent upon the form of ritual being used, he may or may not be required to answer the command "Brother Inner Guard" with a step and sign of the degree.

The Inner Guard is entirely responsible for ensuring that the Candidate is properly prepared for the degree before he is admitted into the lodge room. He should take the greatest care to ensure that the Tyler has carried out the operation of preparing the Candidate for each degree correctly so that when asked by the Worshipful Master "Do you, Brother Inner Guard, vouch that he is properly prepared?" the Inner Guard can answer with absolute certainty "I do Worshipful Master."

The Inner Guard should make himself completely familiar with the various forms of address relating to distinguished visitors so that he may make certain they are correctly announced and thereby accorded the correct protocol required of the occasion.

As this is the first floor office in the lodge it is an occasion for the brother so appointed to show that his formative years as a Steward or lay member have not been wasted.

He should demonstrate that he has prepared himself for office and is both suitably equipped with the requisite knowledge as well as being fully capable of carrying out the duties of that office to which the Master has appointed him.

Poor work on the part of the Inner Guard can mar a ceremony from its beginning. It should always be remembered that in accepting any office in Freemasonry the brother so appointed has a duty to ensure that his knowledge and ability to carry out that role are equal to the task he has accepted.

A quality performance in this junior office will do much to make sure that Brother Inner Guard receives due consideration for higher office when the next Master is elected.

Chapter 5:

To whom does he report?

It has already been stated the Inner Guard receives his instructions from the Junior Warden. There are of course occcasions when he will receive a direct instruction from the Worshipful Master. His line of reporting is of course to the Director of Ceremonies whose responsibilities cover all floor work as well as the planning and execution of all ceremonial within the lodge itself.

Clearly from his position within the lodge room the Inner Guard has a clear view of everything which occurs and equally he himself is clearly seen by all who are present.

It is therefore essential that he communicates both in words and actions all that the requirements of his office and ritual demand, both in a firm clear voice, and with precise signs clearly and properly demonstrated.

The Inner Guard should advise all entrants to the lodge after the meeting has commenced, be they visitors or members, of the degree in which the lodge is operating, in order that they may give the correct signs upon entry. This is not only a courtesy but shows a considerable efficiency in office.

Chapter 6:

When does he leave his post?

An Inner Guard once appointed, invested and installed remains in that post until he is replaced. There is just one occasion which occurs very shortly after his own investiture when he is required to leave his post within the lodge room and that concerns the investiture of the Tyler.

When the Director of Ceremonies advises the Worshipful Master that "Bro ...... has been duly elected as Tyler of the lodge", he follows this by saying, "Is it now your pleasure to invest him?" When the Worshipful Master gives an affirmative reply the Director of Ceremonies moves to the door of the lodge and the Inner Guard opens the door to admit the Tyler.

This then is the occasion when the Inner Guard leaves his post within the lodge room itself, for at this time he should move outside and take over, if only for a short time and on a temporary basis, the duties of the Tyler.

Once the Tyler's investiture has been completed and he leaves the lodge room he will resume his place outside the door and the Inner Guard should then once again take his correct place within the lodge.

The only other occasion when the Inner Guard would normally require to go outside the lodge room is if the occasion should arise where there is no response to his knocks on the door.

The correct action to take is dealt with in a separate chapter later on in this book.

Remember that knocks given by the Inner Guard must always receive a reply; they cannot and must not be ignored by Brother Tyler.

Chapter 7:

Installation Meetings

The occasion of the annual Installation Meeting is a time for considerable extra ceremonial, much of which does not occur during the rest of the masonic year.

Early on in the proceedings of an Installation Meeting the brother who is to be appointed Inner Guard will find that his predecessor is replaced by a Past Master, either of or in the lodge, and on some occasions from an associated or daughter lodge who has been specially invited to the meeting to carry out that task.

The Inner Guard, thus dispossessed, is usually then placed in a vacant chair by the Director of Ceremonies ready for his possible future investiture to a higher office.

When the moment arrives for the new Inner Guard to be taken to the Master's pedestal he should stand when his name is announced and be ready to be taken by the right hand by the Director of Ceremonies after giving him a court bow.

Upon arriving at the pedestal he should at the appropriate moment lower his head to assist the Master in placing the collar of office about his neck. The Master will undoubtedly wish to shake his hand in congratulation of his appointment and investiture. The Inner Guard should respond accordingly.

In some lodges it is customary for the newly appointed and invested officer to salute the Master; in other lodges such is not the case. Local custom and practice should therefore be noted and prevail.

The Inner Guard should complete this part of the ceremony with a court bow to the Director of Ceremonies upon being taken to his seat.

NOTE: A court bow is an inclination of the head, with the body kept perfectly rigid.

Chapter 8:

The First Degree

The reception of a Candidate on the day of his Initiation must surely be an occasion of great importance both to the Candidate and to the lodge. It is therefore essential that this particular ceremony is carried through without any hitch in the proceedings.

In former times it was the custom for the Tyler to give three distinct knocks when presenting a candidate, to make it quite obvious to the brethren in the lodge that it was a candidate at the door and not a brother arriving late. It is to be regretted that this practice has largely disappeared. However, when the Tyler gives the first degree knocks in whatever form is customary, the Inner Guard, taking a step and showing the EA sign which he holds, reports those knocks to the Junior Warden who in turn does the same to the Worshipful Master.

Upon receiving the command from the Junior Warden to ascertain who is outside the door of the lodge the Inner Guard cuts his sign, opens the door and asks the Tyler "Whom have you there?" The Tyler then gives a full and informative reply to which the Inner Guard says "Halt, while I report to the Worshipful Master."

Having closed the door of the lodge the Inner Guard advances, takes a step and gives the sign of the first degree, which he holds, and relays to the Worshipful Master the information he has received from the Tyler.

The Master will undoubtedly reply "Then let him be admitted in due form — Bro Deacons", whereupon the Inner Guard cuts his sign. At this point the Deacons will rise and walk together towards the door of the lodge. When they are approximately six feet from it the Inner Guard should open the door, admit the Candidate and place the point of the p. to his n.l.b., and ask "Do you feel anything?" The Candidate will respond "Yes."

When he is within the porch of the lodge and the Deacons have taken charge of him the Inner Guard should hold above the Candidate's head the Poignard to show that he has been properly challenged.

The ceremony will now proceed according to the ritual used in the lodge. When the O...... has been taken and the Candidate has been escorted to the right of the WM's pedestal the Inner Guard should be ready to perform the next part of his duty.

When the point of the ceremony has been reached where the Master is explaining to the Candidate the symbolism through which he has passed, the Inner Guard should (providing your ritual so states) take the Poignard to the East.

Holding it in his right hand the Inner Guard should, upon reaching the WM's pedestal, place it over his left wrist with the handle facing forwards in order that the Worshipful Master can withdraw it from its holder.

When it is replaced in that holder he should return to his place in the manner detailed by his particular ritual.

When the Candidate is instructed to retire in order to restore himself to his personal comforts the Inner Guard should open the door and allow him to pass out of the lodge into the care of the Tyler.

When a report is received on the door of the lodge the Inner Guard will in the usual manner report this to the Junior Warden who will give a single knock to indicate that the Inner Guard should discover who seeks admission.

The Tyler will announce "The Candidate upon his return."

The Inner Guard makes no reply but closes and locks the door, returns to his position, takes a step, gives the EA sign which he holds, and reports to the Master that it is "The Candidate — Brother ..... on his return". He is instructed to admit him and then cuts his sign and goes to the door.

He should wait until the Junior Deacon is within a few feet of the door before opening it to admit the newly initiated Candidate.

At this point the work carried out by the Inner Guard in the Ceremony of Initiation is concluded.

NOTE: It is we believe highly desirable that the Candidate's name is mentioned to the WM when advising his return. If this is done the suggested format is "WM, the Candidate, Bro ....., on his return."

Chapter 9:

The Second Degree

The work carried out by the Inner Guard in the Ceremony of Passing commences when the Candidate for the degree has answered the questions leading from the First to the Second degree and has been entrusted by the Worshipful Master with the pg and pw leading to the Second Degree.

The Junior Deacon leads the Candidate to the point of address in the north-west where he is instructed to salute the Worshipful Master as an Entered Apprentice Freemason prior to leaving the lodge.

Your role is simply to allow him to retire by opening the door.

The lodge is then opened in the Second Degree, but the knocks are given quietly so as to be audible only in the lodge and you should give the knocks not on the door, but on your l. sleeve whilst standing in your place.

Upon receiving the knocks of the First Degree on the door of the lodge the Inner Guard should rise with a step and the EA sign, which he holds, and advise the Junior Warden that there is a report, which when repeated to the Worshipful Master by the Junior Warden will receive the command "Bro JW, inquire who seeks admission."

The Junior Warden will pass on these instructions, whereupon the Inner Guard should discharge his sign, open the door and enquire of the Tyler "Whom have you there?" The Tyler will reply "Bro ..... who has been regularly initiated into Freemasonry and has made such progress as he hopes will recommend him to be passed to the Degree of a FC, for which ceremony he is properly prepared."

You then ask "How does he hope to obtain the privileges of the Second Degree?" The Tyler will reply "By the help of God, the assistance of the Sq, and the benefit of a pw."

You should say "Is he in possession of the pw?" to which the Tyler should reply "Will you prove him?" You should then ask the Candidate for the pg and pw, and after receiving these correctly, you should say "Halt, while I report to the WM."

You should then close the door, secure it firmly, move to the point of address in the north-west, take a step and salute the WM, taking care to maintain the sign.

Then say "WM, Bro .... who has been regularly initiated into F.........y and has made such progress as he hopes will recommend him to be P..... to the Degree of a FC, for which ceremony he is properly prepared."

The WM says "How does he hope to obtain the privileges of the S...... D......?"

Your reply should be "By the help of God, the assistance of the Sq, and the benefit of the pw."

The Master will reply, "We acknowledge the propriety of the aid by which he seeks admission. Do you Brother Inner Guard, vouch that he is in possession of the pw?"

The reply is "I do, WM", and the WM says "Then let him be admitted in due form — Bro Deacons." You now cut your sign.

At this point the Deacons advance and when they are a few feet from the door you should open it.

When the Senior Deacon has taken charge of the Candidate you should, after placing the Sq to the Candidate's naked breast, hold it aloft for the WM to see that he has been properly admitted.

Your role in the Second Degree is complete apart from allowing the newly passed Candidate out of the lodge and re-admitting him at a later stage when he has restored himself to his personal comforts.

Chapter 10:

The Third Degree

The work carried out by the Inner Guard in the Ceremony of Raising commences when the Candidate for the degree has answered the questions leading from the Second to the Third degree, and has been entrusted by the Worshipful Master with the pg and pw.

The Senior Deacon leads the Candidate to the point of address in the north-west where he is instructed to salute the Worshipful Master as an Entered Apprentice and as a Fellowcraft prior to leaving the lodge.

Your role is simply to allow him to retire by opening the lodge door.

The lodge is then opened in the Third Degree but the knocks are all given quietly in a manner similar to that described for the beginning of the Second Degree.

Do remember that there is a special salutation to be performed at this point before resuming your seat.

Upon receiving the knocks of the Second Degree on the door the Inner Guard should of course advise the Junior Warden that there is a report, remembering to hold the sign.

When it is repeated to the Worshipful Master by the Junior Warden he will receive the command "Bro Junior Warden, inquire who wants admission."

The Junior Warden will so instruct you, by saying "Brother Inner Guard see who wants admission."

You should open the door and enquire of the Tyler "Whom have you there?" and the Tyler will reply "Bro ..... who has been regularly initiated into Freemasonry, passed to the Degree of a Fellowcraft and has made such further progress as he hopes will entitle him to be raised to the sublime Degree of a Master Mason for which ceremony he is properly prepared."

You then ask "How does he hope to obtain the privileges of the Third Degree?"

The Tyler replies "By the help of God, the united aid of the S..... and Cs......, and the benefit of a pw."

You should then enquire "Is he in possession of the pw?" The Tyler replies "Will you prove him?"

You should then ask the Candidate for the pg and pw, and after receiving these correctly you should say "Halt, while I report to the WM."

You then close the door, secure it firmly, and move to the point of address in the north-west, take a step and salute the WM with the MM P Sn, which you must hold and then say,

"WM Bro .... who has been regularly initiated into F..........y, passed to the Degree of a Fellowcraft and has made such further progress as he hopes will entitle him to be raised to the sublime Degree of a Master Mason, for which ceremony he is properly prepared."

The WM says "How does he hope to obtain the privileges of the T.... D......?"

Your reply should be "By the help of God, the united aid of the S. and Cs., and the benefit of a pw."

The Master will reply "We acknowledge the powerful aid by which he seeks admission; do you Brother Inner Guard vouch that he is in possession of the pw?" You reply "I do WM", whereupon the WM says, "Then let him be admitted in due form — Bro Deacons." You now cut your sign and recover.

At this point the Deacons advance and when they are a few feet from the door you should open it and when the Senior Deacon has taken charge of the Candidate you should, after placing the extended Cs. to both bs. of the Candidate hold it aloft for the WM to see that he has been correctly admitted.

Your role in the Third Degree is complete apart from allowing the newly passed Candidate out of the lodge and re-admitting him at a later stage when he has restored himself to his personal comforts.

NOTE: In some rituals the Inner Guard is required to switch on the lights at a given part of the ceremony. You should check with your Director of Ceremonies to make quite sure of the method used in your lodge.

Chapter 11:

Reception of Visiting Brethren

As has already been stated, if the reason behind the creation of the office of Inner Guard is examined we shall of course arrive at the simple answer that the role was created primarily to cover the entry and exit of brethren who wish to join or leave a meeting, as well as ensuring that anyone so presenting himself at the door of the lodge is entitled to admission.

The Inner Guard therefore has a clear duty to make certain that the name and rank of whoever he is asked to admit is stated clearly to the Worshipful Master and, if a visitor, by whom he has been invited.

To enable the Inner Guard to cope with a wide range of titles within the Grand and Provincial rank structures and in order that he may learn their relative positions within these hierarchies, the study of the Masonic Year Book or a copy of a Provincial Handbook is to be highly recommended.

It is sometimes the case that a totally unexpected visitor arrives at the door of the lodge and the helpful Tyler will, if the subject is mentioned to him prior to the meeting, note down the visitor's full name and the rank he holds.

There is nothing to prevent you from reading the name and rank of the brother so presented. Indeed it is far better that the Worshipful Master should be given clear and accurate details of the visitor rather than that he should agree to admit someone whose name has been given wrongly and whose rank was incorrectly stated.

It can sometimes be the case that a visitor from overseas, bearing a letter from the Grand Secretary's office, arrives at the door of the lodge.

This letter addressed to the lodge secretary would advise that Brother...... is visiting the United Kingdom and wishes to attend a lodge operating under our Constitution and that from the information provided there is every reason to believe that the brother so presenting himself is genuine.

The letter will undoubtedly continue that it is the duty of the lodge to ensure that he is properly tested in order that his credibility is established beyond question.

In such a situation the Worshipful Master may well wish to despatch the Director of Ceremonies and a Past Master to examine the brother so presenting himself and to carry out those tests.

After such tests have been concluded the Master should instruct them to return and advise him of the outcome which, if satisfactory, would allow the entry of the brother from overseas.

It is recommended, if such a situation should occur in your lodge, that the brother so presenting himself should be taken to the Worshipful Master by the Director of Ceremonies to receive a personal welcome to the lodge.

Chapter 12:

Reception of a Grand Officer

There may be an occasion when your lodge has a visit from an Officer of the United Grand Lodge of England. Such an Officer should always be referred to as a Grand Officer and never a Grand Lodge Officer.

When this arises, it is absolutely essential that your announcement of that Officer is both accurate and clear to all concerned.

It is frequently the case that, due to the length of the names of some of the ranks within Grand Lodge, confusion occurs in the transmission between the Tyler and the Inner Guard of the name of the Brother and his rank.

It has already been suggested that the writing down of such information is both useful and safe, and this is to be highly recommended should your lodge ever receive a visit from such a high ranking dignitary.

Let us take the situation where you have received only a verbal announcement from the Tyler.

Clearly the brother concerned will be a Past Master and must therefore be a Worshipful Brother. His name will follow, be what it may, and the next part of the announcement will in all probability begin "Past....." followed by the rank to which he has been appointed.

It will prove invaluable to the conscientious and enthusiastic Inner Guard to study and become familiar with the many and varied ranks given in the Book of Constitutions of the United Grand Lodge of England.

Normally there will be a very small range of ranks with which you are likely to have association, but it is essential for you to know where those ranks fit into the overall list of Grand Ranks.

Remember that any active officer of Grand Lodge will have appended to the point of his collar an active rank collar jewel, details of which can also be ascertained from the Book of Constitutions. The jewel will be quite large in size, circular, and have the rank of his office thereon.

Brethren holding past rank have a much smaller oval-shaped jewel attached to the point of their collars.

Although there are a few offices in the United Grand Lodge of England, the holders of which continue from year to year, it is much more usual for an active officer of one year to become a Past Grand Officer upon completion of his year of office.

It should therefore be appreciated that even though you may have a visit from an active officer in the United Grand Lodge of England, it could well be that on the next occasion he visits your lodge, he will have become a Past Grand Officer and should be announced accordingly. ALWAYS look at the collar jewel. If it is oval you can be sure that the wearer holds past rank.

It is worth mentioning at this point that Grand Officers are occasionally promoted from their current rank to a more senior one in Grand Lodge.

It is therefore essential that you never take for granted that a brother, who visited your lodge as a Past Grand Standard Bearer, is necessarily still a Past Grand Standard Bearer. He may well have been promoted to a Past Junior Grand Deacon at the last Annual Investiture of Grand Lodge, and he will not thank you for downgrading him!!!

The simple rule is always check, check, and check again, so that you are not remembered as the Inner Guard who fluffed his introduction of that Grand Officer on the rare occasion that such a visit takes place.

Finally, and most importantly, do not attempt to take a Grand Officer by the hand when he advances into the lodge room. A court bow will suffice to acknowledge this senior officer in Freemasonry.

Chapter 13:

Reception of an Official Visitor

In Provincial and District lodges throughout the United Grand Lodge of England it has become an accepted custom that at least once a year an official visit is made to the lodges under the control of the local Provincial or District Grand Master.

In the case of lodges in the London area such visits are organised by the Grand Secretary's office, and in all cases those brethren who act in the capacity of a visiting officer are specially selected for the task.

In the majority of cases they are Grand Officers whose experience in the craft, gained over many years, has fully equipped them for the role they have been asked to perform.

There are however occasions when a Province or District will use its active and past Provincial and District Grand Wardens for this purpose.

As the Official Visitor, be he from Province, District or from Grand Lodge itself, the brother so designated has a clear role to perform for whoever has asked him to attend and he is both entitled to and deserving of respect and correct treatment during his visit.

It will usually be the case that the Inner Guard has either no part to play or, if any at all, it will be connected with the official visitor's arrival. The manner in which his name and rank should be ascertained has already been described in the previous chapter.

The one advantage that you will have on this occasion is that the name and rank of the 'official' visitor is known well before the day on which the visit is to be made.

You should therefore ascertain from the Director of Ceremonies the details of the brother so attending in order that, should he be delayed, you will be able to announce him correctly to the Worshipful Master who will therefore accord him the dignity to his entrance that his rank demands.

One of the aspects upon which the report of the official visitor will comment is the correct procedures within the lodge and his first contact with those procedures could well be the announcement of his entry by the Inner Guard or in other words you.

Get it right and thereby will begin what it is hoped will be a memorable visit, to say nothing of a creditable report.

Chapter 14:

Reception of a Deputy or Assistant Provincial or District Grand Master

This chapter is specifically written for lodges which form part of a Province or District and are therefore likely to receive a visit from either of the above named senior brethren.

It will occasionally happen that your lodge will be advised it is to receive a visit from the Deputy or Assistant Provincial or District Grand Master for your Province or District.

The protocol which appertains on such an occasion is similar to but no identical to that already described for an official visitor.

The first difference you will notice is that the visiting dignitary will be accompanied by his own Director of Ceremonies who will deal with his entry and exit from the lodge and all matters in which the dignitary is involved while at the lodge meeting.

You will therefore be advised of the name and rank of the Director of Ceremonies and it is he whom you will announce.

This Director of Ceremonies will in turn announce to the WM the person he is accompanying and will form a procession to act as an escort.

Ensure that you have the name and rank of that Director of Ceremonies well learned before the day of the visit so that there is no chance at all of making a mistake.

When the knock is heard on the door you will of course report to the Junior Warden in the usual way and receive from him the instruction to enquire who wants admission.

The Tyler will tell you the name and rank of the Director of Ceremonies accompanying the 'chain' and you in turn will say "Halt while I report to the Worshipful Master".

Upon receiving the instruction to "Admit him Brother Inner Guard" you will do just that.

The Director of Ceremonies will then announce the brother whom he is accompanying with all his styles and titles and 'demand' his admission. Only those holding a patent issued by the

Provincial or District Grand Master, and thereby wear a chain of office, can demand admission.

After receiving the Worshipful Master's agreement to his entry the Director of Ceremonies will form a procession to escort the dignitary into the lodge. This procession usually comprises the lodge Director of Ceremonies and his Assistant the Deacons and the Officers of the Province or District.

It is usual for such Grand Officers who may be present to be invited to join the procession "should they so desire".

Upon the command of the Provincial or District Grand Director of Ceremonies the procession moves off towards the door of the lodge which you will have ready to open at the appropriate point.

NOTE: Where applicable both doors should be opened to afford an easy entry into the Temple.

The last person to leave the lodge room will be the Provincial or District Grand Director of Ceremonies, and it is advisable to close the door to within a few inches so that it is easy to see when the incoming party has been re-formed and the Provincial or District Grand Director of Ceremonies is ready for the procession to re-enter.

Upon the command of the Provincial or District Grand Director of Ceremonies you should immediately open the door fully and allow the full procession to enter the lodge room, after which you should shut and secure it.

The outgoing procession is similarly controlled by the Provincial or District Grand Director of Ceremonies, and as is usual in the case of a normal meeting you should open the door fully to allow the outgoing procession to retire.

Chapter 15:

Reception of a Provincial or District Grand Master

The comments contained in the previous chapter apply equally to the visit, albeit extremely rare, of the Head of a Province or District, namely the Provincial or District Grand Master.

This brother is appointed by the Most Worshipful the Grand Master to preside over the Province or District so designated in his Patent and to appoint such officers as are laid down in the Book of Constitutions Rules 66 to 73, the reading of which will do much to explain the hierarchical structure of such Provinces and Districts.

The brother appointed as a Provincial or District Grand Master is, upon his Installation to that office and rank, immediately accorded the title of Right Worshipful and thereby automatically becomes entitled to a salutation of seven, either within or without his own Province or District. He is also allowed by virtue of his Patent to demand admission into lodges in his own Province or District but not those of other Provinces or Districts.

It is quite usual for the Provincial or District Grand Director of Ceremonies to accompany the head of the Province or District on his visits to lodges.

There really is nothing which should cause the Inner Guard, be he newly appointed or of some service, to worry about his part in the proceedings, providing always that he has done his homework properly and is well prepared before the day of the visit.

The procedure is virtually the same as that already explained for the entry of a Deputy or Assistant Provincial or District Grand Master, both from an incoming and outgoing point of view.

On rare occasions the Provincial or District Grand Master may be accompanied by either one or more members of his executive, such as a Deputy or Assistant Grand Master or Provincial or District Grand Secretary.

If this should be the case they will be included in the announcement made by the accompanying Director of Ceremonies and should give the Inner Guard no cause for concern of any kind.

Chapter 16:

Receiving Right Worshipful and Very Worshipful Brethren

It is possible that a situation will occur during your period of office as Inner Guard when a brother of very senior Grand rank will seek admission into your lodge.

Right Worshipful and Very Worshipful brethren are by their very appointment amongst the most senior members of the Craft and are entitled to a range of salutations above and beyond those normally used and seen in the everyday life of the lodge.

The wise Inner Guard will study Rule 6 of the Book of Constitutions in order to acquaint himself with the ranks of brethren who fall into the groups which are entitled to the prefix of Right Worshipful or Very Worshipful.

In normal circumstances the lodge Secretary would be advised well in advance of the meeting that such a high ranking brother was intending to visit your lodge, and he would plan with the Director of Ceremonies precisely how his reception should be carried out.

The unexpected visit does occasionally happen and it would be sad if the Inner Guard should be found wanting, particularly if this happened in your lodge.

It is certainly the case that within a Province or District the Provincial or District Grand Master will hold the rank of Right Worshipful. His Deputy will usually, but not necessarily hold the rank of Very Worshipful.

In London such lines of demarcation are not so readily available and, as had already been stated, the study of Rule 6 of the Book of Constitutions will not only give clear information, but that knowledge, once committed to memory, will stand the brother in good stead for the rest of his masonic career.

Chapter 17:

What to do if your knocks on the door do not receive a response

It can, and does sometimes happen, that an Inner Guard having given an informative knock on the door of the lodge does not receive a response.

The author has witnessed this on several occasions in his masonic career and in every case the Inner Guard has taken exactly the correct action which is of course to open the door and ascertain why there was a total lack of response.

The reasons for it are many and varied and far too numerous to be entered into here, but if we deal with the fact rather than its cause, what should be done if the Tyler is not to be found?

Clearly the Book, of Constitutions says under Rule 104 (d) that the Tyler is a mandatory office and to hold or to continue a meeting without his presence would contravene this rule. The answer to this problem is simple; it is to report the absence of the Tyler to the Master who will probably appoint a brother from within the lodge (possibly a Steward) to take over the Tyler's post on a temporary basis and until such time as the Tyler returns.

A word of warning – remember that the Tyler may be in a room adjacent to the lodge assisting a candidate to prepare for a ceremony, so allow a reasonable period of time before assuming the absence of the Tyler and unlocking the door, etc, etc.

Chapter 18:

What a brother should know before accepting this office

It may well be the case that having served the lodge as a Steward for a number of years you are pleased if not delighted to be asked to become the Inner Guard by the new Master Elect.

What should your qualifications be to enable you to accept this office and carry it out with credit to yourself and with the satisfaction of the Master who appointed you?

The first few formative years in the lodge should be used to good advantage by a regular attendance at a Lodge of Instruction.

If your own lodge does not have a regular Lodge of Instruction meeting, try to find a lodge working the same ritual which holds a regular weekly meeting at which you would be well received.

By so doing you will quickly become acquainted with the manner of the work and have the opportunity of trying yourself out and also of gaining much satisfaction.

You should never accept the first of the floor offices without a clear and pre-determined intention of progressing through to the Master's chair.

It is very disrupting to the life of the lodge to have a floor officer, and worse still a Warden, drop out after progressing through a number of offices in the lodge.

Think through very carefully your own intentions and when you have reached a decision make a commitment, and make it not only to yourself but also to the lodge.

Try to make that daily advancement in masonic knowledge so that when the day of your Installation as Master arrives you will not only be able to carry out the work contained in the ritual book but will have built up a store of masonic knowledge which will stand you in good stead during your year in charge of the lodge and for your future years in the Craft.

Chapter 19:

What to do when the lodge is "called off" and "called on"

The one and only occasion when you should not knock on the door immediately after the Worshipful Master has given a single knock is when the lodge is "called off" and/or "called on". On all other occasions you will of course simply repeat the knocks of the Junior Warden. Why should this be?

The small piece of ritual which accompanies the "calling off" or "calling on" of the lodge gives us the answer to that question for the Junior Warden is so instructed by the Master who says "I will thank you to declare it" or some equally similar command.

At the "calling on" the Master says once again to the Junior Warden "I will thank you to declare it" or again some similar command.

On each occasion the Junior Warden knocks once with his gavel followed by the Senior Warden and then the Master.

The Inner Guard should take no action whatsoever.

THE
DEACONS

Chapter 1:

Historical Preface

The Origin of the word 'Deacon'

The word is derived from the Greek '*diakonos*' and the Latin '*diaconus*', meaning servant, waiting-man, helper or messenger.

The English term 'deacon' was in use in the days of James 1 but the masonic term comes to us, not through English, but through Scottish tradition.

At one time the Church deacon was a lay officer (as he still is in some denominations) and his duties were more those of an almoner.

The word is found in many continental languages, having been derived from an ancient Greek word meaning 'servant' and carrying with it the suggestion of 'running' and 'pursuing' hence the idea of 'messenger'.

In the Scottish operative lodges, the Deacon came to be in many cases the chief officer, his duties being quite different from those of a Deacon in a speculative lodge today.

His jewel clearly suggests that his duty was that of a messenger.

In the eighteenth century the Deacon's jewel, or emblem, was often a figure of Mercury with winged feet and helmet, his left foot on a globe and his left hand holding a caduceus. It was the wand of the 'ancient' herald, especially that carried by Hermes, the messenger of the gods, the conductor of the dead to the lower world and the patron of travellers, orators, and (let us tell the whole truth) thieves!

Since the founding of the United Grand Lodge of England the Deacon's jewel in its lodges has been a dove with olive branch, and emblem believed to symbolize the messenger sent from the Ark by Noah.

For a full and comprehensive description of that history of the Deacon's wand the reader would be well advised to refer to the relevant chapter in *The Freemasons Guide and Compendium* by the late Bernard Jones.

The earliest reference to the Deacon in an English lodge is 1733 though obviously their duties were undertaken prior to that by some member of the lodge designated for that purpose.

The first time they are mentioned in terms of Grand Deacons is 1814.

Chapter 2:

The Office

Few would deny that any meeting of a lodge without the presence and active participation of the Deacons would be incomplete.

So necessary have they become to our proceedings that the late Bro. Sinclair Bruce, PJGD, chose to make them the subject of his Prestonian Lecture in the year 1985, which was entitled ".....not only Ancient but useful and necessary Officers..... THE DEACONS."

For the purpose of assisting both Junior and Senior Deacon in their highly differing roles I have dealt with their duties separately thereby giving to each the individual treatment which those two roles so rightly deserve.

The role of the Deacon brings the holder of that office into contact with every officer in the lodge and it has often been said that a good deacon usually make a good Master.

Some words of advice to every aspiring deacon — move with dignity and grace, hold your wand vertically about 12 inches from your body, look calm and organised, control your candidate with care and consideration, take your time throughout the ceremonies, do not get flustered, and never, never, rush any part of your duties.

Chapter 3:

The Duties of the Office

It is usually agreed that the Deacons are very important officers in the lodge.

Certainly it is true that the floor work performed by them forms a very large part of each of the ceremonies conducted in craft masonry today.

A Deacon performing his duty well can leave a permanently favourable impression on the candidate he is conducting, whereas a Deacon performing his duty poorly will leave the candidate with a feeling of unease and apprehension.

One duty which properly carried out is a joy to watch is the changing of the Tracing Boards. Poorly or clumsily handled it becomes nothing less than a shambles and does the image of the lodge very little good.

There would appear to be little, if any, tuition given in this simple but important part of the meeting, and this subject is therefore dealt with in a completely separate chapter such is its importance.

When carrying out floor work in any degree it is of the utmost importance that the two Deacons can and do work together in a well planned and cohesive manner.

It takes considerable practice to achieve this degree of perfection and aspiring Deacons should spend time with their opposite partner is ensuring that they work as a pair and not as two separate individuals no matter how will they perform on their own.

Chapter 4:

The Installation Meeting

I shall begin the instruction for the Junior Deacon from the moment the collar and jewel of office are placed around his neck at the Installation meeting and he is taken to his place by the Director of Ceremonies.

He should upon being placed in front of his chair give the Director of Ceremonies a court bow, sit, and then place his wand in the stand adjacent to his chair, not the other way round.

You are now the Junior Deacon and should be ready for any call upon you to perform in that new role.

What then will be your first duty? Very probably to assist in closing the lodge by turning the First Degree Tracing Board to face the Junior Warden's pedestal.

It does sometimes occur that the closing of the VSL involves the Deacons and if this should be the case in your lodge it is usual for the wands to be crossed before the IPM leaves his place to perform that part of the ceremony.

The next function you will perform is to participate in the outgoing procession and very probably be included in that procession as the first officer to be "collected" by the Director of Ceremonies and Assistant Director of Ceremonies during their first perambulation around the lodge.

You will be joined by your fellow deacon as you pass around the north-east corner and he should be allowed to move in front of you to the inside of the procession. This must be agreed with him beforehand, so that is is done in a dignified manner.

Moving off together you will proceed to the south where you will move past the Junior Warden's pedestal and then stop whilst the Director of Ceremonies escorts the Junior Warden from his post to a position in the procession immediately behind you as Junior Deacon.

The procession will move off again and proceed past the Senior Warden's pedestal where once again it will stop whilst the Director of Ceremonies conducts the Senior Warden from his post and places him behind the Senior Deacon.

Once again the procession will move off. The Senior and Junior Wardens will stop in the north-east part of the lodge whilst the rest of the procession proceeds on to a position between the pedestals of the Junior Warden and Senior Warden where it will halt upon the command of the Director of Ceremonies.

The Worshipful Master will be escorted by the Director of Ceremonies to a position behind and between the Senior and Junior Deacons, and his Wardens will be instructed to form themselves behind the Master. Grand Officers, Past Grand Stewards, Provincial or District Grand Officers and Holders of Senior London and London Grand Rank and Overseas Grand Rank, will then be invited to join the outgoing procession.

The Director of Ceremonies will then say "Forward brethren" and the procession will move towards the door of the lodge room where the Director of Ceremonies and the Assistant Director of Ceremonies and the two Deacons will stop, turn inwards so as to allow those following to pass between them. At this time the two Deacons raise their wands and remain in that position until all the participants in the procession have left the lodge room.

Your first meeting as Junior Deacon of the lodge is over.

Chapter 5:

The Ceremony of Initiation

There can surely be no greater feeling of satisfaction than that experienced by the Junior Deacon on the occasion of his receiving and conducting a Candidate for initiation through that ceremony.

I shall start at the point where the Worshipful Master says "Then let him be admitted in due form Brother Deacons."

The Senior Deacon will, dependent upon the ritual used, either move directly to the north-west or square the lodge, join you, and then proceed to the door of the lodge which will be opened by the Inner Guard.

There before you will be the Candidate, ready for his entry into the lodge, and your first charge who will rely on your care and consideration throughout the ensuing ceremony.

The Inner Guard having applied the point of the p. will hold it aloft to show that the entry of the Candidate has been correctly handled according to the ritual, and you will gently place your left arm under the right arm of the Candidate and guide him slowly to the point of address in the north-west, quietly whispering to him to halt when he is in the correct position.

The Worshipful Master will now say, "Mr......., as no person...... age of twenty-one years?" The candidate, prompted by you, should answer "I am".

The Worshipful Master will speak again "Thus assured, I will thank you to kneel . . . our proceedings."

You should now very quietly whisper to the candidate that there is a kneeling stool right in front of him and you should place him gently in a position whereby he can easily kneel down.

The Deacons, holding their wands in their left hands, cross them over the head of the Candidate and give the sign of R...... There is no need for the Candidate to give the sign of R...... for it will be meaningless to him at this time.

The Worshipful Master then delivers the P..... and continues "In all cases of .... put your trust?" The Candidate, prompted by you, replies "In..."

The Worshipful Master then instructs the Candidate to rise and follow, etc., etc. You should at this point assist him to rise and once again place your left arm under his right arm holding him by the wrist or the hand in a firm but not tight grip.

The Worshipful Master continues with a preamble before ending with the words "... proper person to be made a Mason."

You should now whisper quietly to the Candidate to step off with his left foot and gently take him around the lodge, squaring it in the north-east and south-east, finally arriving in the south.

Instruct the Candidate to move sideways to his left.

A gentle but firm grip on his wrist will indicate that he should now stop.

The ceremony of interchange with the Junior Warden can now take place.

You will gently take the Candidate's hand and tap thrice on the right shoulder of the Junior Warden.

He will begin by saying to you "Whom have you there?" to which you reply "Mr..... a poor Candidate in a .... etc ... Freemasonry." The Junior Warden continues "How does he hope to obtain those privileges?" You reply "By the help .... and of good report." The Junior Warden says "Enter, free and of good report."

You then move gently to the right ensuring that the Candidate is quite clear of the tracing boards before instructing him (quietly) to step off with his left foot. You then proceed to the Senior Warden where precisely the same investigation is carried out.

After the Senior Warden has completed his part of the exchange you should once again instruct the Candidate to move to the right.

When he is clear of the kneeling stool instruct him once again to step off with the left foot and take him to the left-hand side of the Senior Warden, who having remained standing will address the Worshipful Master saying "WM I present to you Mr...... a Candidate properly prepared to be made a Mason."

The Worshipful Master addresses the Senior Warden ending with the words "... will answer with candour".

At this point the Senior Warden restores the Candidate's right hand to you, and once again you should place your arm under his right arm and hold his wrist firmly but not tightly.

Move on to the edge of the carpet and stop, at the same time telling him in a whisper not to say anything until he is instructed by you.

The Worshipful Master will then proceed to put the usual questions to the Candidate, and you will instruct him to answer each of the three questions with the words "I do."

When this has been completed the Worshipful Master will address the Senior Warden, who in turn will then tell you to "... instruct the Candidate to advance to the ped..... in due form."

At this point you will instruct the Candidate in an audible voice to move off slowly commencing with his left foot.

You should stop him in a position appropriate to the space needed to perform the next part of the ceremony. This can usually be estimated at between five to six feet from the Master's pedestal.

> NOTE: It is usually the case that the Candidate will take a much smaller step than you believe he will. It is therefore a wise Junior Deacon who makes a suitable allowance for this.

You should now move in front of the Candidate and take his left hand in your right hand whilst retaining his right hand in your left hand.

Slowly but deliberately draw him towards you, telling him in a whisper to step off with his l.f.

When you have reached a position where the Can. is directly in front of and in line with the Worshipful Master tell him to place his feet together.

When he has done this, tell him to turn out his right foot to form a square. Some Candidates find difficulty in doing this so you must be prepared immediately to adjust the position of his right foot if necessary.

Then instruct him to take a short pace with his left foot, and at the same time move your right hand which is holding his left hand to approximately the position you wish him to complete that step. You will find that he will do precisely that.

Next instruct him to complete the step by drawing his right foot after it.

Proceed to complete this part of the ceremony by dealing with the other two steps in a similar manner, endeavouring to arrive at the ped. exactly at the point where the third step is completed.

The Can. should now be almost touching the kneeling stool which should be far enough away from the ped. to allow him to kneel in comfort without having to bend backwards.

The Worshipful Master will now address the Can. who will require a prompt from you in the appropriate place in order to be able to answer the Worshipful Master's question, to which the correct response is "I am."

The Worshipful Master will then instruct the Can. to kneel on his l.k. with his r.f. formed in a square, and then will instruct him to give him his right hand which he will place on the open VSL.

The Can. is then handed a pair of Cs. one point of which is presented to his nlb. You should be ready to raise and guide the Candidate's hands to the appropriate positions. Make certain that the free arm of the Cs. hang downwards.

You should make quite sure at this point that the Can. is comfortable and not suffering any distress, bearing in mind that he is wearing a hoodwink.

Holding your wand in your left hand you will now raise it in front of that of the Senior Deacon so that the wands are crossed above the head of the Candidate.

You should now stand to order with the step and sign of the First Degree.

The Worshipful Master then commences the Obl...... with the preamble "Repeat your name at length and say after me..." The remainder of this part of the ceremony will continue as shown in the book of ritual used in your lodge.

At the words "...my G and SO of an EA Freemason" having been repeated by the Can. both you and the Senior Deacon should lower your wands to your rh sides.

The Worshipful Master will remove the Cs from the Can's left hand and the Senior Deacon should lower the left hand of the Can. to his left side. The Can's right hand remains on the VSL until he is raised by the Worshipful Master.

The Worshipful Master then continues "What you have repeated etc....... on the VSL."

The Can. will generally do so without prompting but should this not be the case then you should indicate by gentle pressure on the back of his head that you wish him to bend his head slightly forward.

When this has been completed the Worshipful Master will say "Having been kept....., etc, predominant wish of your h....?"

The Can. prompted by you will reply "L....t." The Worshipful Master will then instruct you to carry out this action whilst he suits his actions to the occasion.

The h..k having been removed, the Can's head should be directed forward gently so as to bring the VSL into his direct line of sight.

The Worshipful Master then explains the three great lights in Freemasonry and concludes by raising the Can. by his right hand.

You should, once he is standing, place your left arm under his right arm and lead him to the right hand side of the Worshipful Master.

The Worshipful Master will now give the explanation of the three lesser L...ts, followed by the presentation and explanation of the p., and the explanation of its significance and use in the ceremony of Initiation.

The explanation of the ct is then given, followed by the meaning and purpose of the Ob.........n.

The Can...... is then instructed by the Worshipful Master to take his first regular step in F..y.

You should quietly whisper to the Can. to do exactly as you do and then proceed to show him the correct manner of placing his lf with his rh into its hollow.

The Worshipful Master will then proceed to explain the significance of this part of the ceremony which will lead automatically into the explanation of the s... of the degree.

Although the Worshipful Master will tell the Can. to copy him you should be ready to assist the Can. to carry out this part of the ceremony correctly.

The interchange between the Worshipful Master and the Can. (prompted by you) will then take place including the sharing of the w. This part of the ceremony will conclude with the Worshipful Master saying "Pass..."

The Worshipful Master will now pass the Can's right hand to you and once again you should place your left arm under his right arm.

Do not move until the Worshipful Master is seated, at which point you are free to move in front of the ped. and instructing the Can. to step off with his lf move towards the south-east corner of the lodge where he should be instructed to square the lodge and then pass down to the south.

You should stop at the left hand side of the Junior Warden's ped. and then instruct the Can. to move sideways to his left so that he arrives at the right side of the Junior Warden.

You will then salute the Junior Warden with the step and s.... of the degree and say "Bro JW, I present to you Bro... on his initiation."

The Junior Warden will reply "I will thank Bro... to advance to me as a Mason."

The Can., prompted by you, will take the step and show the sn to the Junior Warden who will then say "Have you anything to communicate?"

The Can. should be prompted to reply "I have."

Upon communicating the G. the Junior Warden will say "What is this?" to which the Can., prompted by you, should reply "The G or Tn of an EA FM."

The Junior Warden will then ask "What does...... demand?" The Can. should reply "A ...." whereupon the Junior Warden will say "Give me that ...." and the Can. will then reply prompted by you, "At my initiation I......etc....with you."

It is imperative that the Can, should be prevented from saying the word.

The Junior Warden will say "Which you please and begin". When this interchange is completed the Junior Warden will say "Pass....."

A similar but slightly extended version of this communication section of the degee is undertaken at the Senior Warden's ped.

In each part of this exchange you will lead the Can. into his part by prompting him with the words to use and ensuring that he does not speak until you have so provided the correct words for him to say.

The method of arriving at the right hand side of the Senior Warden is identical to that used for the Junior Warden, as is the method of starting the dialogue with the Senior Warden.

When the Senior Warden has spoken the words "Pass...." you should take the Can. to the left-hand side of the Senior Warden's ped.

Place the right hand of the Can.... in the left hand of the Senior Warden, who will then face the Worshipful Master and with the s... and s... of the degree say, "WM I present to you Bro...... on his initiation, for some mark of your favour."

The Worshipful Master will reply "Bro. SW, I delegate you to invest........ of a Mason".

The Senior Warden complies with that instruction, at the conclusion of which he retains hold of the right hand corner of the A.... in his l h and then says to the Can. "Bro ... by the Worshipful Master's command............it will never disgrace you."

The Senior Warden will then hand the care of the Can. back to you as Junior Deacon and then resume his seat at which point you should place the Can. a few paces in front and to the left of the Senior Warden's ped. facing east.

The Worshipful Master will then address the Can. "Let me add to the observations of the............should be disturbed by your presence."

The Worshipful Master then addresses you as Junior Deacon "Brother Junior Deacon you will place our.......of the L...."

You should then instruct the Can. to step off with his l f, and proceed to take him slowly down the north part of the lodge stopping about four to six feet from the north-east corner.

You then say to the Can. "l f across the lodge, r f down the Lodge, pay attention to the WM." You may now release his hand. Make certain that the Alms Dish has been placed where you can easily pick it up when required.

The Worshipful Master then proceeds to give the Charge which starts "It is customary, at the erection of all stately........ (and concludes) ...it will be thankfully received and faithfully applied."

At this point you will move to a position approximately three to four feet in front of the Can. and proffer the Alms dish whilst saying the words "Have you anything to give in the cause of Charity?" Should the Can. not reply you should proceed quickly to the second

The Deacons

question "Were you deprived of everything of v...... previously to entering the Lodge?"

The Can. must reply to this question of his own volition, and you then say "If you had not been so deprived would you give freely?" On receiving his reply in the affirmative, you then face the Worshipful Master give the s... and s..., and say "WM, our new made Brother affirms that he was d......d of everything v..l..e previously to entering the Lodge or he would give freely."

The Worshipful Master then addresses the Can. again commencing with the words "I congratulate you on the honourable sentiments......... the opportunity of practising that v....e you have professed to admire."

When this passage has been completed by the Worshipful Master you should once again take the Can. by placing your left arm under his right arm and conduct him in an arc to the front of the Worshipful Master's ped, where the Worshipful Master will give a full explanation of the w...... t.... of the first degree.

Immediately after this the Worshipful Master will continue with the explanation of the lodge Warrant, which he will display, and finally present to the Can. a copy of the Book of Constitutions and By-laws of the lodge.

The Can. is then advised that he may retire to restore himself to his personal comforts, and after the Worshipful Master (or whoever has been conducting the ceremony) shakes him by the hand, you are free to conduct him to the north-west corner of the lodge where he should be instructed to salute the Worshipful Master with the s... and s... of the degree.

When this is completed he should be taken to the door of the lodge which will be opened by the Inner Guard and he should then be handed into the care of Bro. Tyler.

After a brief interval the knocks of the degree will be given on the door and these will of course be answered by the Inner Guard. The Worshipful Master will then give you instructions to admit the Can. whereupon you should automatically rise and move towards the door which will not be opened by the Inner Guard until you are in position and ready to receive the Can. once more.

Having received him and once again taken him by the right hand and arm, you should move to the point of address in the north west and instruct him to make the s... and s... of an EA FM.

Rituals vary widely in stating the position of the Can. when the charge is being delivered. In some he remains where he is placed in the north-west, whilst in others the Worshipful Master will say "Bro. Junior Deacon place our Bro. in the centre of the lodge".

If the latter system is used in your lodge, then after placing him in that position you should retire to your seat leaving the Can. on his own in the centre of the lodge whilst the Charge after Initiation is given.

When the words "From the very commendable attention ..." are reached you should slowly move forward until standing a pace behind the Can.

You can, upon the completion of the Charge, once again take him by the right arm and conduct him straight to the seat on the Senior Deacon's right, where with a court bow you may leave him to sit down.

You now return to your own seat in the lodge.

NOTE: If there are two Candidates for initiation, the Senior Deacon will be responsible for the second candidate. In such cases the Director of Ceremonies will arrange the procedure according to the practice of the lodge.

Chapter 6:

The Second Degree

I shall begin the work of the Junior Deacon in the Second Degree at the point where the WM notes that the next item on the agenda is the Ceremony of Passing.

The Worshipful Master will then go on to say "Brethren, Bro.... is this evening a Candidate to be passed to the Second Degree... I shall therefore proceed to put the necessary questions."

As Junior Deacon you will leave your seat and proceed to collect the Can. and take him to the point of address in the north-west part of the lodge.

The Worshipful Master will then proceed to ask him the questions leading from the First to the Second Degree.

The answers should be forthcoming from the Can. without the need for any prompting, but if he is nervous or is overcome by the occasion you may well have to supply him with a prompt.

You must therefore be ready to supply that prompt if needed, but please ensure it is given in a whisper.

Let us now assume that this part of the ceremony has passed off without any problem.

At the conclusion when the Worshipful Master says "These are the usual questions etc., etc., etc., ... to do so", you should proceed with the Can. along the north part of the lodge to the north side of the Worshipful Master's pedestal. You should place him, and stand yourself, about one pace away from the Worshipful Master but facing the s.....

The Worshipful Master will then ask him two questions the answers to each being "I do" which you will prompt the Can. to give as a reply.

He will then be entrusted by the Worshipful Master with the pg and pw leading from the First to the Second Degree.

You should be ready to assist by telling him to repeat the pw given by the Worshipful Master who will conclude this part of the ceremony with the words "Pass, ..."

You should now take the Can. to the north-west corner of the lodge where he should be instructed to salute the Worshipful Master as an EA FM.

The Can. should now be taken to the door of the lodge where the Inner Guard will allow him to pass out to the Tyler for preparation for the Ceremony of P....g.

The lodge is now opened in the Second Degree.

The Tyler gives the knocks of an EA on the door and the Inner Guard reports appropriately to the Junior Warden, after which the Worshipful Master instructs that the Can. be admitted and adds "Brother Deacons."

The control of the Can. in this degree is of course in the hands of the Senior Deacon, but there are some important points for the Junior Deacon to note since his participation in the success or otherwise of this degree is very much dependent upon the ability of the two deacons to work together as a cohesive unit.

Upon the entry of the Can. into the lodge the Senior Deacon takes charge of him and takes him to the point of address in the north-west.

The Can... is instructed to salute the Worshipful Master as an EA FM.

The Junior Deacon should take up a position on the left side of the Can. whilst this is taking place.

Upon the instruction from the Worshipful Master for the Can. to kneel the Deacons hold their wands in their left hands and cross them above the head of the Can. showing the S... of R..... with the right hands.

When the p..... is completed the Deacons should drop the s... and return their wands to their sides.

It is the duty of the Junior Deacon to remove the kneeling stool at this point by moving it to the left.

When the Senior Deacon and the Can. have started to perambulate the Junior Deacon should place the kneeling stool back in front of the Senior Warden's pedestal and then resume his seat.

Your next participation in the ceremony of P...... is at the point where the Can. is instructed by the Senior Deacon how the steps of the degree are to be taken.

You should time your arrival at the Worshipful Master's pedestal so that you reach the north-east part of the lodge just as the Senior Deacon and the Can. complete the steps of the degree, so that all three of you are in a straight line, the Junior Deacon on the left, the Can. in the centre, and the Senior Deacon on the right.

The worshipful Master then advises the Can. about another O........ and will ask him if he is willing to take it.

The Can. replies prompted by the Senior Deacon.

The Worshipful Master instructs the Can. how to kneel, and you as the Junior Deacon will be required to hold the Sq.... in place on the Can's. left elbow.

When the Can. is comfortable and in the correct position the Worshipful Master will gavel and the Deacons should raise their wands above the head of the Can. the Senior Deacon's in front. Only the Senior Deacon will be able to show the Sn of F.

The ceremony continues until the point where the Worshipful Master will indicate that he wants the Sq... removed and will hold out his hand to receive it.

At this point you should place the Can.'s left hand down to the side of his body.

Upon the instruction given by the Worshipful Master "Rise newly O....... FC FM" the Senior Deacon will wheel the Can. round in a clockwise circle to the right hand side of the Worshipful Master. This will allow you to return to your seat along the south side of the lodge.

Your work in this degree is now at an end.

If the explanation of the second degree tracing board is to be given it is possible that the Worshipful Master will require the use of your wand to indicate the various features of the board to the Can. in which case be ready both to give it to him and receive it back at the conclusion of the lecture.

NOTE: If there are two Candidates for passing, you will be responsible for the second Candidate. In such cases the Director of Ceremonies will arrange the procedure according to the practice of the lodge.

Chapter 7:

The Third Degree

I shall start at the point at which the Junior Deacon first becomes involved in the ceremony of Raising. This occurs immediately after the lodge has been opened in the T.... D.....

The Tyler gives the knocks of the FC on the door and the Inner Guard reports appropriately to the Junior Warden after which the Worshipful Master instructs that the Can. is admitted and adds "Brother Deacons."

The control of the Can. in this degree is of course in the hands of the Senior Deacon. There are however some important points for the Junior Deacon to note since the success or otherwise of this degree is very much dependent upon the ability of the two Deacons to work well together.

Upon the entry of the Can. into the lodge the Senior Deacon takes charge of him and takes him to the point of address in the north-west part of the lodge.

The Can. is instructed to salute the Worshipful Master as a Fellow Craft, first as a EA.

At this point, the Junior Deacon should take up a position on the Candidate's left.

Upon the instruction from the Worshipful Master for him to kneel, the Deacons cross their wands above the head of the Can. and then show the S... of R..... with their right hands.

When the p....r is completed the Deacons should drop the s. and return their wands to their sides.

It is the duty of the Junior Deacon to remove the kneeling stool at this point by moving it to the left.

When the Senior Deacon and the Can. have started to perambulate, the Junior Deacon should place the kneeling stool back in front of the Senior Warden's pedestal and then resume his seat.

NOTE: It should be noted here that in the Emulation
            working the Junior Deacon follows closely behind the
            Senior Deacon and Can. and that the act of replacing
            the stool is carried out by the I.G.

When the Can. is handed by the Senior Deacon to the Senior
Warden for presentation to the Worshipful Master the Senior
Deacon will take up a position to the left of the Can. and the Junior
Deacon should move to his left.

Your next participation in the ceremony of R..... is at the point
where the Can. is instructed by the Senior Deacon how the steps of
the degree are to be taken.

You should time your arrival at the Worshipful Master's
pedestal so that you reach it just as the Senior Deacon and the Can.
complete the steps of the degree, so that all three of you are in a
straight line, the Junior Deacon on the left, the Can. in the centre,
and the Senior Deacon on the right.

The Worshipful Master than advises the Can. about another
O........ and asks if he is willing to take it.

The Can. replies, prompted by the Senior Deacon, and the
Worshipful Master instructs him how to kneel.

When he is comfortable and in the correct position, the
Worshipful Master will gavel and the Deacons should raise their
wands above the head of the Can. the Senior Deacon's in front,
taking the Sp and MM PSn.

The ceremony continues until the point where the Worshipful
Master explains the position of the Sq. and Cs.

Upon the instruction given by the Worshipful Master "Rise
newly O....... M.M." the Senior Deacon will with your assistance
remove the Can. back a few paces to the edge of the g.

The retrospect is then given by the WM who finally says "Bro.
Wardens."

The Wardens then leave their respective posts, go to their new
positions, and take over the care of the Can. from the Senior
Deacon and you.

At this point you should either retire to the west or return to your
seat. This will depend entirely upon the working used by your
lodge.

The Senior Deacon will take charge of the Can. when the
Worshipful Master has concluded the explanation of the Sns.... and
Wd.... of the degree.

The Can. will be instructed to salute the Worshipful Master in all three degrees and will then retire from the lodge.

Your work in this degree is now at an end.

NOTE: If there are two Candidates for raising, you will be responsible for the second Candidate. In such cases the Director of Ceremonies will arrange the procedure according to the practice of the lodge.

Chapter 8:

Preparation prior to your appointment

Any meeting of a lodge is an opportunity to learn or to practise the duties of a lodge officer and this applies as much to the office of Junior Deacon as any other.

The wise and forward-looking officer will always be using the opportunity to study and watch the work of the other officers of the lodge.

The smooth and trouble-free working of the Deacons will only be possible if the floor movements are rehearsed and rehearsed until they can be carried out without any prompting from others.

Much has already been written about the manner in which the right hand and arm of the candidate should be held by placing your arm under that of your charge.

It will be readily appreciated, when this is tried for the first time, just how effective this one simple action can prove to be.

If the candidate's hand is taken in such a manner that your hand and arm are over the top of the candidate's, you have little control and your candidate cannot be directed into precisely the position you require him to go.

It is a wise Deacon who tries both methods if only to establish the benefit of one over the other.

Your audibility is something which requires to be checked.

Ask a friend in the lodge to tell you whether or not you can be heard when you speak your various parts in the ceremonies.

For some people who are not used to speaking in public, the ability to speak clearly and project their voice is an art which has to be learned.

It requires the benefit of a tutor and plenty of practice before an acceptable level of performance can be reached.

Never take it for granted that your voice is audible all over the lodge; the greater the audience the louder you have to speak.

It is a feature of the speech of some people that they tend to drop their voice at the end of a sentence, and the words thus spoken are therefore lost to the assembled brethren.

Such features of speech can be rehearsed at the Lodge of Instruction where you will receive sound advice, plus coaching and correction with regard to your own projection and performance.

It is always a good idea to attend the meeting early (about forty-five minutes before the start is a good time) in order that you can pace out exactly where you wish the candidate to start and stop in the various degrees. There is no substitute for rehearsal and practice.

Such pre-planning and thought will undoubtedly be an advantage, for it is by such sound forward-thinking that your own performance will improve and your confidence will grow.

The various parts of the ceremony should come together to please not only you or the Worshipful Master who appointed you, but the Past Masters and other members present including the visiting brethren.

In the first degree always ensure that someone has been delegated to pass the alms box or bag to you at the appropriate point in the ceremony. Nothing should ever be left to chance for you do not want to experience a 'nasty moment' whilst brethren dash around to rectify situations which should have been thought of prior to the start of the meeting.

The success or otherwise of any meeting will depend to a large degree upon the thought and planning which has gone into the occasion well before it commences and certainly well before the day itself. Think and plan ahead; it always pays dividends.

One of the joys of holding the office of Deacon is that your work in that office of necessity brings you into contact in an operative sense with all the other officers who are involved in the conduct of the ceremonies from the Inner Guard through to the Master.

Such close contact will of course have its considerable advantages in the sense that whilst learning your own part in the ceremonies which are to be carried out, you will automatically learn a growing proportion of those sections carried out by other officers.

This is a feature of the floor work as every former Deacon will testify.

Use your two years as a Deacon wisely for they will enable you to grow not only in ability, but also in stature within the lodge, and you will become proficient in the overall work of the lodge.

As with most things in life you very quickly discover that the more you learn the more there is to learn.

Chapter 9:

The Tracing Boards

The heading of this chapter may seem at first sight a little superfluous, for what possible difficulty can there be in turning tracing boards around so that the correct board is showing. However, there can be problems.

For the benefit of those who have never tackled this part of the duty of the Junior Deacon let us go through this apparently simple action in detail so that once learned it will never be forgotten.

Rituals as well as lodges differ widely, so that in some the changing of the tracing boards is the duty of the Junior Deacon whilst in others that same role is given to the Senior Deacon.

Further, in some lodges because the wands of the Deacons are ceremonial items, it is considered that they should be carried only in the ceremonies and not when performing routine duties such as changing the tracing boards. You should be careful always to conform to the practice of your lodge.

The following facts apply equally to whoever is entrusted with the duty.

Tracing boards should be checked prior to the start of the meeting to ensure that they are in order, with the Third Degree tracing board nearest to the Junior Warden's pedestal followed by the Second Degree tracing board and then the First, all facing towards the south.

When the appropriate part of the ceremony is reached where the tracing board needs to be turned around to show its front, you should turn the board clockwise and replace it in its original position.

This is a simple action and is quite straight forward to carry out.

When the Second Degree tracing board requires to be shown, take both the First and Second Degree tracing boards by the top and turn both around in a clockwise direction and replace them in their original position.

Moving to the Third Degree we should take all three tracing boards by the top centre and turn all three together and replace them in their original position.

When the Master wishes to resume the lodge in the Second Degree you should once again take all three tracing boards and turn them around in a clockwise direction replacing them as before.

Having reached that point in the proceedings where the lodge is either closed in the Second Degree or resumed in the First Degree you should take just two tracing boards and turn them once again in a clockwise direction.

When the lodge is finally closed and the end of the meeting has been reached you should then turn just one tracing board which will ensure that all three boards are facing the Junior Warden's pedestal.

The shuffling of tracing boards with one being placed behind and between others which is so often seen in lodges is both unnecessary and looks untidy, and should therefore be avoided.

Try practising these movements for they really are much easier to carry out than you might at first realise. They will bring to the action of tracing board changing a new dimension and a freshness of approach.

The writer appreciates that there are cases where some very old tracing boards are in use which are of a size and weight which would not allow for the actions as indicated to be carried out.

These, however, are few and in the majority of cases the turning of tracing boards can be carried out by a brother using one hand.

If it is the practice in your lodge that the Deacon takes his wand with him when changing the tracing board then you should retain the wand in your right hand and change the Tracing Boards with your left. If this is likely to prove difficult, it may be better to allow someone to hold your wand whilst changing them. Remember that dignity is essential in this just as much as any other part of the proceedings.

A final word on the subject of tracing boards.

There are many lodges in which the tracing boards are placed in front of the pedestals of the Junior Warden, Senior Warden and Master respectively and once uncovered they are left that way until the lodge is resumed in the lower degree when they are once again turned to face the pedestal. In such cases the Senior Deacon is usually responsible for the tracing board in front of the Master's pedestal and the Junior Deacon for the other two.

Some Directors of Ceremonies are adamant that a tracing board of a lower degree must not be on show once the lodge has moved to a higher degree; such, however, is most definitely not the case.

It is based on the incorrect assumption that when a lodge has been opened, for example in the second degree, it is closed in the first. That is not so. It is open in both degrees.

The information given in this chapter is of course directed only to those lodges in which the tracing boards are placed in front of the Junior Warden's pedestal.

There are many in which a central box or table is used, and there are some lodges where the boards are mounted on one of the walls.

Clearly where such individuality exists it would be wrong to change it.

Chapter 10:

Co-operation between Deacons

Co-operation is a very easy word to say but a difficult action to undertake unless it is entered into by the parties concerned with a complete commitment on both sides.

They must ensure that the conjoint work in which they are involved is rehearsed and rehearsed until they automatically perform their various roles with a polish and efficiency which is the admiration of all who are privileged to witness them.

Such co-operation and its resultant effect upon the manner in which the ceremonies are performed will prove that no matter how well an individual officer learns his part his interface with the other members of the team is as important, if not more important, that an outstanding performance on the part of one individual.

As with any team effort the end result is what counts, and it is as a team that a lodge builds itself for the future. The officers who make up a lodge team have a duty to themselves and to the Worshipful Master who appointed them to perform their duties efficiently and as perfectly as they are able.

Knowing your part in the ceremony and knowing it well is pointless unless you know the parts which the other officers have to play.

As you progress through to the chair of King Solomon you will become more and more able to identify the roles of the various officers and the places at which they interlink with your own.

To learn the ceremonies in Freemasonry from your own standpoint and from that standpoint alone is showing a lack of consideration for the overall team of which you are a member.

Therefore when considering the word 'co-operation' remember it is indeed a word which is easy to say but requires a genuine and dedicated commitment on your part if it is to be transmitted into action.

Chapter 11:

The Senior Deacon
The Ceremony of Initiation

I shall start at the point where the Worshipful Master says "Then let him be admitted in due form, Brother Deacons."

The Senior Deacon will, dependent upon the ritual used, either move directly to the north-west or square the lodge and join the Junior Deacon. He will then proceed to the door of the lodge which will be opened by the Inner Guard.

The Inner Guard having applied the point of the p...... will hold it aloft to show that the entry of the Candidate has been correctly carried out according to the ritual.

The Junior Deacon will take charge of the Can. and place him in the appropriate position.

The Worshipful Master will now say "Mr.........., as no person...... age of twenty-one years?" The candidate, prompted by you, should answer "I am."

The Worshipful Master will then say "Thus assured, I will thank you to kneel..... our proceedings."

Your duty at this time is to take a position at the left of the Can. and at the correct moment raise your wand above his head.

The Worshipful Master then delivers the P..... and continues "In all cases of .... put your trust?" The Candidate, prompted by you replies "In... .'

The WorshipfulMaster then instructs the Candidate to rise and follow, etc., etc., etc.

The Worshipful Master continues with a preamble before ending with the words "...proper person to be made a Mason."

You should now withdraw the kneeling stool to the left and when the Junior Deacon has commenced his perambulation you should replace that kneeling stool in the proper position in front of the Senior Warden's pedestal.

When this has been completed you should return to your seat.

NOTE: In the Emulation ritual the Senior Deacon takes the
p.... to the Master's pedestal at this point.

When this has been completed the Worshipful Master will address
the Senior Warden, who in turn will then tell you to "...instruct the
Candidate to advance to the ped..... in due form."

When the Junior Deacon has carried out the ceremonial required
to arrive at the Worshipful Master's pedestal you should take up
your position on the left of the Can.

The Worshipful Master will then instruct him to kneel on his lk
with his rf formed in a square, and then instructing the Can. to give
him his right hand the Worshipful Master will then place it on the
open VSL.

The Can. is then presented with a pair of Cs., one point of which
is presented to his nlb whilst the other point hangs downwards.

You will now raise you wand and place it behind that of the
Junior Deacon so that the wands are crossed above the head of the
Can.

You should now stand to order with the step and sign of the First
Degree. (Some rituals say the S... of F.......).

The Worshipful Master then commences the Obl...... with the
preamble "Repeat your name at length and say after me...", and
the rest of this part of the ceremony continues as shown in the book
of ritual used in your lodge.

When the words "...my G. and S.O. of an EA FM" have been
repeated by the Can. both you and the Junior Deacon should lower
your wands to your r.h. sides.

The Worshipful Master will remove the C.s. from the Can's left
hand and you should lower the left hand of the Can. to his side.

After the Worshipful Master has explained the three great lights
in Freemasonry and concluded by raising the Can. by his right
hand, you should turn and resume your seat.

After the perambulations around the lodge have been completed
by the Junior Deacon the Can. will arrive at the pedestal of the
Senior Warden, where he will be presented to the Worshipful
Master and subsequently be invested with his apron and instructed
to move to the south-east of the lodge. The Junior Deacon will show
him the position in which he must stand.

NOTE: In some workings it is customary for the Senior Deacon to take up a position to the left of the Can. at this point. In others the Senior Deacon takes up this position just prior to the alms dish being proffered. In Emulation working the Senior Deacon remains in his seat.

Your part in the ceremony of Initiation is now at an end.

NOTE: If there are two candidates for initiation you will be responsible for the second candidate. In such cases the Director of Ceremonies will arrange the procedure according to the practice of your lodge.

Chapter 12:

The Second Degree

I shall begin the work of the Senior Deacon at the point where the Worshipful Master notes that the next item on the agenda is a Ceremony of Passing.

He will then say "Bro..... is this evening a Candidate to be passed to the Second Degree... I shall therefore proceed to put the necessary questions."

The Worshipful Master will then do so, after which he will entrust the Can. with the pg and pw leading from the First to the Second degree.

This part of the ceremony will conclude with the words "Pass......."

The Can. is now shown out of the lodge, into the care of the Bro. Tyler.

The lodge is then opened in the Second Degree.

The Tyler gives the knocks of an EA on the door and the Inner Guard reports appropriately to the Junior Warden after which the Worshipful Master instructs that the Can. be admitted and adds "Brother Deacons."

Upon the entry of the Can. into the lodge the Senior Deacon takes charge of him and conducts him to the point of address in the north-west part of the lodge, where he is instructed to salute the Worshipful Master as an EA FM.

Upon the instruction of the Worshipful Master for the Can. to kneel, the Deacons cross their wands above the head of the Can. and give the sn of R. The Senior Deacon should instruct him to show the sn of R........ with his right hand.

When the p....r is completed the Deacons should drop their s... and return their wands to their sides.

It is the duty of the Junior Deacon to remove the kneeling stool at this point by moving it to the left.

You should now assist the Can. to rise, and then by taking him in the usual manner start to perambulate the lodge, saluting the Worshipful Master as you pass.

Upon reaching the Junior Warden the Can. should be instructed to advance as a EA FM showing the Sn and communicating the Tn and Wd.

The Junior Warden will say "Have you anything to communicate?" The Can. should be prompted by you to reply "I have."

The method of communication should then by given by the Can. but with your supervision to ensure it is done correctly. The Junior Warden will then say "What is this?"

You will instruct the Can. to reply "The G. or Tn of an EA FM."

The Junior Warden will say "What does it demand?".

The Can. prompted by you should reply "A. ......"

The Junior Warden will respond with "Give me that .... freely and at length."

The Can. prompted by you should comply.

The Junior Warden will reply "Pass ....".

You will now instruct the Can. to move to the right by a series of sideways steps until he is clear of both the Junior Warden's pedestal and the tracing boards, at which point you instruct him to step off with his left foot until you reach the Senior Warden's pedestal.

Upon passing the Senior Warden you should instruct the Can. to salute him as an EA FM.

Having arrived at the point of address in the north-west of the lodge you should stop.

The Worshipful Master will at this point speak to the Brethren, and when this is concluded you will once again perambulate the lodge saluting the Worshipful Master and Junior Warden as an EA FM in passing.

Arriving in the west you should instruct the Can. to advance to the Senior Warden showing the Sn and communicating the pg and pw he received from the Worshipful Master previously to leaving the lodge.

The Senior Warden will say after this has been done "Have you anything to communicate?" to which you will instruct the Can. to reply "I have."

The Senior Warden will respond with "What is this?"

You will instruct the Can.... to respond "The pg leading from the First to the Second Degree."

The Senior Warden says "What does this pg demand?"

The Can. responds "A pw."

The Senior Warden says "Give me that pw."

The Can. prompted by you complies with that request.

The Senior Warden says "What does ...... denote?"

Once again the Can. responds.

The Senior Warden then says "How is it usually depicted in our Lodges?"

(NOTE: some rituals say in a Fellowcraft lodge)

The Can. should respond with "By an e o c near to a f of w."

The Senior Warden will then say "Pass ..." and replace the Can..'s right hand in your left hand. You should then conduct the Can. to the north of the Senior Warden's pedestal and place his right hand in the left hand of the Senior Warden who will present him to the Worshipful Master, after which you will be told to instruct the Can... to advance to the E in due form.

The Worshipful Master then advises the Can. about another O........ and asks if he is willing to take it.

The Can. replies prompted by you.

The Worshipful Master instructs the Can. how to kneel and you should take a Sq (usually from the IPM) and pass it behind the Can. to the Junior Deacon.

When the Can. is comfortable and in the correct position the Worshipful Master will gavel and the Deacons should raise their wand above the head of the Can., the Senior Deacon's in front. Only you will be able to give the Sn of F.

The ceremony continues until the point where the Worshipful Master will indicate that he wants the sq... removed and will hold out his hand to receive it from the Junior Deacon.

The Worshipful Master will then explain the position of the S..... and Cs....... in the Second Degree after which he will then say "Rise duly O....... FC FM."

You will then wheel the Can. around in a clockwise direction to the right hand side of the Worshipful Master.

The Worshipful Master will then proceed to entrust the Can. with the secrets of the Degree.

Having been so entrusted by the Worshipful Master he will then call the Can. to repeat the w.... This should be carried out by the Can. after being so instructed by you.

When this is completed the Worshipful Master will say "Pass ...."

The Can. must now be taken to the right hand side of the Junior Warden, where after giving the s... and s... of the degree you will start the exchange by saying to the Junior Warden "Bro. Junior Warden, I present to you Bro. ...... on his being passed to the Second Degree."

The Junior Warden will reply "I will thank Bro. ..... to advance to me as FC FM." The Can... should do so under your instruction showing the s... and s... of the degree.

The Junior Warden will then say "Have you anything to communicate?" to which the Can... should reply (under your guidance) "I have."

The G... of the degree should then be given by the Can., but it is your duty to ensure that he communicates it correctly.

The Junior Warden will then say "What is this?" to which you should prompt the Can... to reply "The G. or Tn. of a FC FM."

This will be followed by the Junior Warden saying "What does it demand?" to which the Can. should say "A word."

The Junior Warden replies "Give me that word." The Can. suitably replies and then says "I will l.... or h.... it with you." The Junior Warden responds with "Which you please, and begin."

When the communication has been completed the Junior Warden says "Pass ...."

A similar discourse is undertaken at the Senior Warden's pedestal, culminating with the words by the Senior Warden "Pass ......"

The Can. should now be brought round to the left of the Senior Warden who will take his right hand, raise it, face the Worshipful Master and say "W M, I present to you Bro. .... on his being passed to the Second Degree for some further mark of your favour."

The Worshipful Master responds with "Bro. Senior Warden, I delegate you to invest him with the distinguishing ..... of a FC FM."

The Senior Warden then removes the Can's apron and replaces it with that of a FC FM.

The Senior Deacon can and should assist the Senior Warden in this action.

It is essential that it should be done in a dignified manner, preferably by the Senior Warden taking the EA apron and placing it on one side just a second before the Can. is invested with the FC apron. The exact procedure to be followed should be agreed with the Senior Warden beforehand.

The Senior Warden then says "Bro. ..... by the Worshipful Master's, command... etc. etc." concluding with the words "...in the science."

The Can... will be handed back to you by the Senior Warden and you should place him at the point of address.

The Worshipful Master will address the Can. concluding with the words "...wonderful works of the Almighty."

He then says "Bro... Senior Deacon, you will place our Brother in the SE part of the Lodge."

You will now proceed with the Can. along the north side of the lodge and square the north-east corner, crossing over and squaring the south-east corner and then stopping, whilst the Can. is placed correctly in position about four to six feet from the south-east corner of the lodge.

You should then say to the Can. "R F across the Lodge, l f down the Lodge, pay attention to the WM."

The WM then proceeds to explain that Masonry is a progressive science and continues through to the words "...mysteries of Nature and Science."

You should then take the Can. by the right hand and in a clockwise arc take him to the Worshipful Master's pedestal where the Worshipful Master will proceed to explain the w t of a FC FM.

When this explanation has been completed you should take the Can. to the point of address and instruct him to salute the Worshipful Master as a FC, first as an EA, prior to leaving the lodge.

When this has been completed the Can. should be taken to the door of the lodge and handed into the care of the Tyler in order to restore himself to his personal comforts.

When the knocks of the degree are received the Inner Guard will then take the appropriate action to advise the Junior Warden who will instruct the Inner Guard to admit the Can.

You should without any instruction move to the door of the lodge to bring in the Can.

When he is once more inside he should be instructed to salute the Worshipful Master as a FC, first as an EA.

If the lecture on the Second Degree Tracing Board is to be given, you as Senior Deacon will very probably be instructed to place the Can. in the centre of the lodge at the foot of the Tracing Board of the degree. The brother delivering the lecture may wish to borrow your wand while he does so, but this is something that should be decided before the meeting.

If this is the case in your lodge you should remain with him throughout this part of the ceremony, at the conclusion of which you should recover your wand, then escort him to the seat immediately to the right of your own, give him a court bow and sit.

If the Second Degree Tracing Board is not to be given, you should take the Can. immediately to the seat allocated for him after he has saluted the Worshipful Master.

Your participation in the Second Degree is at an end.

NOTE: If there are two Candidates for passing the Junior Deacon will be responsible for the second Candidate. In such cases the Director of Ceremonies will arrange the procedure according to the practice of your lodge.

Chapter 13:

The Third Degree

I shall start the work of the Senior Deacon in the Third Degree at the first point at which he becomes involved in the ceremony of Raising.

This is after the lodge has been opened in the S.... D..... and the Worshipful Master has announced that there will be a ceremony of R...... .

You should leave your chair and proceed to collect the Can. and place him at the point of address in the north-west of the lodge.

The Worshipful Master will generally prefix his entry to the ceremony with the words "Bro ..... is this evening a Can. to be raised to the T.... D.... but it is first requisite that he gives proofs of his proficiency in the Second."

The questions from the Second to the Third Degree will then be asked and answered with (if necessary) a gentle prompt from you.

When this has been completed you will conduct the Can. to the right hand side of the Worshipful Master's pedestal where he will be entrusted with the pg and pw leading from the Second to the Third Degree.

You should repeat the words immediately after the Worshipful Master has said them and then ensure that the Can. does the same.

At the conclusion of this entrustment the Can. should be taken to the point of address where he should be instructed to salute the Worshipful Master before leaving the lodge first as a EA then as a FC.

When this has been completed the Inner Guard will open the door and the Can. may be handed into the care of the Tyler for preparation for the ceremony of R...... .

The Tyler gives the knocks of the S.D. on the door and the Inner Guard reports appropriately to the Junior Warden who in turn reports to the Worshipful Master.

The Worshipful Master will then direct the Inner Guard to admit the Can. in due form and will add "Bro. Deacons."

The control of the Can, in this degree is entirely in the hands of the Senior Deacon from this point onwards.

Upon the entry of the Can. into the lodge the Senior Deacon takes charge of him and the Inner Guard uses both points of the Cs. in the established manner, afterwards raising them to show the Worshipful Master that this part of the ceremonial has been complied with correctly.

The Can. is taken by you to the point of address in the north-west part of the lodge, when he is instructed to salute the Worshipful Master as an FC, first as an EA.

The Junior Deacon should take up a position on the left hand side of the Can. whilst this is taking place.

Upon the instruction from the Worshipful Master for the Can. to kneel the Deacons cross their wands above the head of the Can. instructing him to show the Sn. of R.

Both Deacons then show the Sn of R themselves with their right hands.

When the p....r is completed the Deacons should drop the Sn and return their wands to their sides.

It is the duty of the Junior Deacon to remove the kneeling stool at this point by moving it to the left.

When the Senior Deacon and the Can. have started to perambulate the Junior Deacon should replace the kneeling stool in front of the Senior Warden's pedestal and then resume his seat.

NOTE: It should be noted here that in the Emulation working the Junior Deacon follows closely behind the Senior Deacon and Can. and that the act of replacing the stool is carried out by the Inner Guard.

You should now proceed with the Can. in the time honoured manner along the north side of the lodge, squaring the north-east corner.

The Can. should be instructed to salute the Worshipful Master as an EA in passing.

Proceed to the south-east corner which should be squared and then move along the south side of the lodge until you reach the right-hand side of the Junior Warden.

You should instruct the Can. to halt at this point and then ask him to move to the left in a side stepping motion until you reach the right hand side of the Junior Warden.

You now say to the Can. "Advance to the Junior Warden as such, showing the Sn and communicating the Tn. and Wd."

The Junior Warden will say "Have you anything to communicate?" You should now instruct the Can. to say "I have."

The Junior Warden will then say "What is this?"

You will instruct the Can. to reply "The G or Tn of an EA FM."

The Junior Warden will say "What does it demand?"

The reply should be "A ...."

Junior Warden "Give me that .... freely and at length."

You should instruct the Can. to give the ..... .

The Junior Warden will then say "Pass ...."

You will tell the Can. to move approximately three or four steps to the right.

When you are sure that he is clear of both the pedestal and the tracing boards you should instruct him to step off in the usual manner.

After squaring the lodge in the south-west you will pass the Senior Warden and in doing so you should tell the Can. to salute the Senior Warden as a Mason in passing.

You will arrive back at the point of address.

Without waiting for any prompt whatsoever you will once again move along the north side of the lodge and square the lodge in the north-east as before.

You will now instruct the Can. to "salute the Worshipful Master as a FC in passing."

When this has been done you will arrive at the south-east part of the lodge which should of course be squared and then proceed along the south side of the lodge.

When you pass the Junior Warden you should instruct the Can. to salute him as a FC in passing.

In the south-west you should once again square the lodge.

Arriving at the right-hand side of the Senior Warden you should instruct the Can. to move sideways to the left with three or four short steps.

When you are in position you should say, "Advance to the Senior Warden as such showing the Sn and communicating the Tn and Wd of that Degree."

The Can. should then take the Sp and show the Sn... of the Second Degree and then cut it.

The Junior Warden should then say "Have you anything to communicate?" and the Can. (prompted by you) should reply "I have."

The Senior Warden will then test the Can. and say "What is this?" to which he should receive the answer from the Can. (again prompted by you) "The G or Tn of a FC FM." Continuing, the Senior Warden will say "What does it demand?" to which the reply by the Can. should be "A ..."

The Senior Warden will then say "Give me that ...., freely and at length."

When this has been done the Senior Warden will say "Pass ...."

You will now take the Can. carefully by the right hand and instruct him to step sideways three or four steps to the right ensuring that he is clear of the kneeling stool at the front of the Senior Warden's pedestal and then proceed to the point of address in the north-west part of the lodge where you should halt.

The Worshipful Master will now address the brethren of the lodge ending with the words "...properly prepared to be raised to the sublime Degree of a MM."

This is your signal once again to start a perambulation by proceeding along the north side of the lodge until you reach the north-east, where once again you will square the lodge.

On passing the Worshipful Master's pedestal you will instruct the Can. to salute the Worshipful Master once again as a FC in passing.

After squaring the south-east corner you should instruct the Can. to salute the Junior Warden once again in the same manner, and upon arriving in the south-west corner square the lodge as previously.

Move to the same position on the right-hand side of the Senior Warden as you did in the previous perambulation, and instruct the Can. to move sideways as before until arriving at the right-hand side of the Senior Warden.

You should tell the Can. now to "Advance to the Senior Warden as such showing the Sn and communicating the pg and pw you received from the Worshipful Master previously to leaving the lodge."

The Senior Warden will say after receiving the aforementioned communications "Have you anything to communicate?" and the Can. (prompted by you) will say "I have."

When this exchange has been completed the Senior Warden will say "What is this?" The Can. (again prompted by you) will reply, "The pg and pw leading from the Second to the Third degree." The SW will enquire "What does this pg demand?" and the Can. should say "A pw."

The Senior Warden will respond with "Give me that pw." The Can. should reply with the correct response after which the Senior Warden will say "What was ......?"

The Can. should reply "The first a in ms." The Senior Warden's final question will be "The import of the ...? and the Can. will reply "..... ...."

Finally the Senior Warden will say "Pass ...."

The Senior Warden will now restore the rh of the Can. to you which is your signal once again to instruct the Can. to move sideways to the right and also once again to ensure he is clear of the pedestal of the Senior Warden and the kneeling stool.

Move to the left-hand side of the Senior Warden placing the Can's rh in the lh of the Senior Warden. You should then move to the l of the Can.

The Junior Deacon will now join you on your left-hand side.

The Senior Warden will present the Can. to the Worshipful Master who will in turn say "Bro Senior Warden you will direct the D's to instruct the Can... to advance to the E by the proper steps."

This instruction will be repeated to you by the Senior Warden.

You will now carry out that part of the ceremony which demonstrates to the Can. the method by which he can advance from the W to the E in this degree.

When this has been completed you will be standing at the front of the WM's pedestal with the Junior Deacon arriving at exactly the right time on the left of the Can.

When the Can. is in position the WM will address the Can. and end with "Are you prepared to meet them as you ought?" You should prompt the Can. with "I am."

The WM will then instruct the Can. how he should k.... and place his ha...s on the VSL.

The Ob...... is then taken by the Can. which ends with the words "...this is my solemn Obl.... of a MM."

All present should cut the P Sn at this point and the Deacons should lower their wands.

The Can. is then required to seal his Obl.... on the VSL after which the attention of the Can. is called to the position of the S and Cs.

The Worshipful Master removes the Can's rh from the VSL and raises him, after which he hands him into your care, and you should now conduct him back to the foot or edge of the g.

The Worshipful Master will now deliver the exhortation ending with the words "The manner of his death was as follows, Brother Wardens."

The Wardens then advance and take over the position of the Deacons.

At this point the Deacons should turn outwards and return to their seats.

NOTE: In some rituals the Deacons remain on the floor of the lodge assuming a position at the top edge of the g.... almost in line with the Junior Warden's pedestal.

The Worshipful Master then proceeds with the ceremony of the Third Degree, and the next time you are required is at the completion of the explanation of the Sns and Wds of the degree when the Worshipful Master says "You are now at liberty to retire" etc. etc. etc. ending with "...will be further explained" whereupon the W.M. returns to his seat.

At this juncture you will have been sitting for quite a long time but you must ensure you are ready immediately, and without prompting, to resume your role at this point in the ceremony.

You once again take charge of the Can. this time for the purpose of escorting him to the point of address in the north-west, where he salutes the Worshipful Master in all three degrees prior to leaving the lodge and being released into the care of the Tyler.

NOTE: In some rituals the Deacons stay with the Can.
        throughout the full explanation of the Sns and Wds
        being communicated by the WM and participate in
        the s. and s. of the degree.

NOTE: In some rituals all three s.... are given in full but in
        others including Emulation only the P. S. is given.

When the Can. has been restored to his personal comfort and the
required report has been given and received, the Worshipful
Master will say to the Inner Guard "Admit him."

You will receive no instruction or prompt at this point but you
should be ready to proceed automatically to the door of the lodge to
receive the Can.

Having received him you should take him to the point of address
in the north-west where he should be instructed to salute the WM
in all three degrees, full s.... in every degree.

When this is completed the Can. should be wheeled around and
handed into the charge of the Senior Warden.

After the Senior Warden has invested the Can. with the badge of
a MM he will hand the Can.... back to you by his rh. As in the
previous degree, the investiture should be done in a dignified
manner and the way in which you assist the Senior Warden should
be agreed with him beforehand.

You should once again proceed to the point of address and halt
whilst the Worshipful Master speaks to the Can. ending with the
words "...in the inferior degrees."

You should then proceed with the Can. to the front of the
Worshipful Master's pedestal by whichever route is required by
your ritual.

The WM will now deliver the Traditional History.

It is important that you instruct the Can. to copy you at the
appropriate points in this address.

The WM will proceed to the explanation of the Third Degree
Tracing Board, after which he will explain the other s.... in this
degree which should also be copied by the Can. under your
instruction.

The conferring of the degree will be complete when the WM
utters the words "...where the world's Great Architect lives and
reigns for ever."

You should now show the Can. to a seat to the right of your own.
Your work in the ceremony of the Third Degree is now complete.

NOTE: If there are two Candidates for raising the Junior
       Deacon will be responsible for the second Candidate.
       In such cases the Director of Ceremonies will arrange
       for the procedure according to the practice of your
       lodge.

Chapter 14:

Public Speaking

The two year period of office that a brother serves as a Deacon can have a secondary advantage for those who are prepared to think ahead and plan their path through to the chair of King Solomon.

It is frequently the case that the delivery of the addresses in a lodge are given in the main to the more senior members, and in the majority of cases these fall to Past Masters.

The interested brother will take every opportunity that comes his way to learn the art of speaking and improve with every chance he gets.

The Master of the lodge is very often at a loss to know whom to ask to propose various toasts at the Festive Board and in particular the toasts to the guests or the Past Masters and Officers of the lodge. An approach to the Master will be readily and enthusiastically accepted.

If the number of meetings which the lodge holds during the course of the working year is thought of as a number of opportunities to experiment and improve your performance, you should eventually arrive at the Master's chair with a background of experience and knowledge.

Remember that speaking at a masonic Festive Board is a totally different experience from engaging in public speaking on any other occasion.

For the benefit of the Inner Guard or Deacon who is looking ahead and planning his future let us then go through the process of the Festive Board from start to finish so that you can slowly become acclimatised to the various sections which go towards the total procedure with which we are all so familiar.

Possibly the most usual mistake which occurs to a newly installed and inexperienced Worshipful Master is to launch into the Toast List which presumably has been placed ready for his use by Brother Secretary.

What then is wrong with that? It is very often the case that the list so produced starts with the first 'official toast' namely that to the Queen and the Craft, which indeed that toast most certainly is. What has been forgotten is that before we start the list of toasts we must above all make quite sure that we ask the Brethren to stand in order to sing or say 'Grace'.

We have already stated that the first toast is to the Queen and the Craft, and in the United Kingdom this must be given first.

In countries outside the United Kingdom where the United Grand Lodge of England has lodges operating under its auspices it is very often the custom for the first toast to be to the Head of State of that country, and this is accepted as being quite the correct procedure to adopt.

Presuming that we are dealing with the usual rather than the rare the toast to the Monarch and the Craft would be taken as the first toast of the evening and would therefore be the first to receive masonic fire if this is given in your lodge.

Just one small point worth mentioning at this stage which is that the order of announcement, singing of the National Anthem, toasting and fire are quite clearly laid down by the United Grand Lodge of England in precisely that form. The order therefore is, Announce, Sing, Toast, Fire.

Quite obviously if the National Anthem is usually sung within the lodge room it must not be repeated at the Festive Board.

Remember that the Official Toast List laid down by Grand Lodge consists of a continuous series of toasts, and long gaps between each toast are to be avoided.

Not only does this delay the departure of the guests but it is also inconsiderate for those brethren who may have long journeys to make to return to their homes.

We should now proceed to the second toast of the evening which is to the Most Worshipful the Grand Master, (currently) His Royal Highness the Duke of Kent.

Smoking may now be permitted.

The next toast is to the Pro Grand Master by name, the Deputy Grand Master by name, the Assistant Grand Master by name and the rest of the Grand Officers present and past.

Please note that the term Grand Lodge Officers should never be used and should be corrected if ever it should occur in your lodge. The correct terminology to use is Grand Officers.

You may perhaps have a Grand Officer present and, as matter of courtesy, you might ask him to respond. He may or may not wish to do so.

Should there be more than one Grand Officer present, then the senior officer should always be asked first and if he declines he may suggest that the next most senior officer be asked.

You will of course know the ranks of the Grand Officers by this time for you will have studied them as recommended earlier in this book.

Let us therefore presume that this part of the proceedings has passed off correctly. What then follows this toast?

In a Province or District it would be the toast to the Provincial or District Grand Master. If in London it would be the toast to Holders of Senior London Grand Rank and London Grand Rank.

If the Provincial or District Grand Master is present it is virtually certain that he will respond to his own toast.

Where the toast is given in London the Master may or may not request a response. In some London lodges the response is given just once a year. In other lodges it takes place at every meeting. The response must be by a holder of that rank, not by a Provincial Grand Officer no matter how exalted his rank.

The next toast will be to the Deputy and Assistant Provincial and District Grand Masters and Officers of the Province or District in which the meeting is being held. Any response must be by an Officer of that Province.

The toast which follows is that to the Master which is usually, but not necessarily always, given by the Immediate Past Master.

In some lodges this toast is given only on Installation nights but in most lodges it is given at each meeting of the lodge, and it is therefore a wise IPM who plans what he is going to say at each meeting throughout the year.

He will obviously wish to present a different facet of the Master and be non-repetitive in his approach. Much can be gained from the master's wife with regard to his other interests which would come in useful as content for your speech if and when you find yourself in that situation.

The response by the Master will give him the opportunity to make such announcements as he feels he wishes to make concerning the lodge and the programme of events he has planned for the year. He may also wish to use the occasion to talk about his particular charity and give some specialised information concerning its activities.

We now move to the toast to the Initiate which should always be given by a senior member, preferably a Past Master of the lodge, for such is the importance of the occasion that we should impress on the Candidate just how highly we regard the entry of a new member to our Order. The Candidate will then reply.

The next toast is to the Visiting Brethren, which once again should be entrusted to a skilled and capable brother for such is the importance we place on brethren from other lodges visiting us.

We must show them in the most tangible way possible that we are both pleased to see them and trust that have not only enjoyed their visit but will wish to attend our lodge again at some time in the future.

Dependent upon the custom of the lodge one or more replies may well be requested from those who have attended, but once again be sure that protocol is observed and the most senior guest is asked to reply first.

The next toast is to the Past Masters and Officers of the Lodge, and this is the opportunity for a younger and inexperienced brother to begin public speaking by taking the chance to deliver a few words of respect to his seniors in the lodge, perhaps taking the opportunity to thank those who have helped him in his masonic career to date.

Seldom is it the case that this speech needs to be of more than a very few minutes duration but it does allow the brother so delivering it to stand, speak, call for the fire and get used to the whole experience of standing and speaking in public.

It may be that for the first few occasions he has to use a written script, but it will build his confidence and that should be the object of asking a junior member of the lodge. It is all part of preparation for eventual higher office.

The occasion now presents itself to honour a toast to "Absent Brethren". This requires no speech unless of course there is a particular reason for so doing.

Finally the Master will call for the Tyler's toast with a double knock of the gavel.

The Tyler will give his toast in the usual and accepted manner finishing with asking all present to join in masonic fire, taking the time from him.

We have gone through the list of toasts very carefully so that the reader may note just how each toast follows its predecessor and see the variations which are allowed, as well as the protocol which should be used in connection with seeking replies from brethren of senior rank.

A final piece of advice for the future. It is frequently the case that at an Installation Meeting the lodge will provide an entertainer to sing the Master's song. Such an artist may well return to give a little more entertainment at a later stage in the proceedings. It will be your duty when you are the Master to ensure that such entertainment does not continue beyond a reasonable and pre-determined period of time.

The Master of a lodge has the care of ALL his brethren to consider, be they old, young, senior or junior. The excitement of the occasion, particularly if it is the Installation Meeting, must never be allowed to overshadow the well-being and consideration of all brethren.

Chapter 15:

Balloting

During the course of any masonic year the act of balloting in its various forms is undertaken by every lodge. The simple act of placing a ballot ball into a ballot box appears at first sight to be the most simple of procedures to undertake but there are opportunities to fail and in some cases to fail badly.

Let us for the sake of the record deal with the various occasions in which a ballot becomes necessary and the Deacon is usually involved.

The Worshipful Master and the Treasurer

The manner of balloting usually adopted for electing the Master and the Treasurer is by the completion of a slip of paper for each office.

These slips of paper are usually distributed by the Deacons and then, after completion by the members of the lodge, are collected by the Deacons and handed to the Master for verification.

It is totally unnecessary for the Master or anyone else to read out each slip of paper. All that the Master is required to do is to announce the name of the person who received the majority of the votes cast.

We would caution against the use of the word 'unanimous' for two simple reasons. Firstly because it is virtually impossible to be sure that every brother who was entitled to vote has done so. Secondly the statement itself is totally unnecessary to the proceedings. Further, it would be very embarrassing indeed if the Master was accustomed to using the word 'unanimous' but had to omit it if there were one or two adverse votes.

These same comments apply equally to the ballot for the Treasurer.

The Tyler

The usual manner of electing the Tyler is by a show of hands after a proposal, which does have to be seconded, has been made in open lodge. The Master should announce the result of the ballot which must be recorded by Brother Secretary.

Honorary Members

The Book of Constitutions rule 167 clearly states the manner in which the ballot for an Honorary Member must be conducted, namely by individual ballot and be declared 'carried' unless three or more black balls appear against it.

It is therefore imperative that the brother, who has been so designated to deal with the allocation of the ballot balls, shall be instructed to place only one ball into the palm of each member of the lodge, excluding of course existing Honorary Members.

If the black and white ball system is used in your lodge obviously one ball of each colour should be handed to each member who is to participate in that ballot.

It is often the case that a brother, who has not been so correctly instructed, is seen to proffer to each member the full bag of ballot balls from which the member could quite easily take two or three without anyone being aware. Such an action could easily lead to an improper ballot with the resultant animosity within the lodge.

It is a useful and helpful action if the experienced Deacon ensures that the newly appointed Deacon is made aware of this method of distribution of ballot balls and the reasons which lie behind it being carried out in that particular manner.

Initiates and Joining Members

The same procedure is adopted as is used in the balloting for the Honorary Members, namely a choice of a yes or no drawer.

Once again the brother handling the ballot balls to the lodge members should be very careful to ensure that each brother receives only one ball for each ballot unless of course the black and white ball system is being used.

Combined Balloting

It is not generally appreciated that it is perfectly permissible for a combined ballot to be taken for a Joining Member and an Initiate.

The United Grand Lodge of England recognises only 'Candidates' not as is often incorrectly presumed Candidates for a specific reason i.e. Initiation or Joining. If as a result of a conjoint ballot being taken it proves not to be in favour, then a separate ballot must be taken immediately to determine the separate results.

A final thought is given on the use of the ballot box. It is often the case that in an endeavour to assist members of the lodge to vote 'Yes' the Deacon carrying the ballot box is seen to tilt the box at an angle to facilitiate the voting member easier access to the 'Yes' drawer.

It must be remembered that it is equally as democratic to vote against a resolution as to vote for it.

Tilting a ballot box in either direction is to be deprecated, and when it occurs it should be stopped without delay.

Deacons should not carry their wands during a ballot unless it is an established custom of the lodge.

Chapter 16:

Processions

Although the act of walking into and out of the lodge with your fellow Deacon can hardly be called difficult, there are a number of points which if watched very carefully and rehearsed prior to the meeting can and will impart an extra polish to the way in which you both carry out your duties.

Deacons like most other officers come in various sizes and the way in which they carry their wands will be different every year. Even assuming that we have two Deacons of equal height, it is almost a certainty that when asked to pick up their wands, each will both raise their individual wand to an entirely different height from the other.

Practice is therefore necessary, indeed essential, if we are to have some system of ensuring that the two Deacons can and do work as a team. It is a very simple matter to secure the assistance of another officer in the lodge to act as an arbiter to ensure when the two wands are being lifted from the floor that both officers are able to achieve the same height time and time again.

Further, in processions, the senior should always be on the right of the junior and as, in the outgoing procession, the junior will join the procession first, it is essential that a dignified way for the senior to join it should be well rehearsed beforehand.

As in all matters in Freemasonry, rehearsal is the way to achieve perfection. To maintain perfection requires constant practice.